The Road to Wholeness

# THE ROAD TO WHOLENESS

## LAURA A. MATHIS, Ph.D.

Tyndale House Publishers, Inc.
Wheaton, Illinois

Cover illustration by Roy Pendleton.

Excerpt reprinted with permission from Ann Landers, News America Syndicate, and the *Wisconsin State Journal*.

Excerpt reprinted from *Profiles in Courage* by John F. Kennedy, copyright 1956, Harper and Row, New York, New York 10022. Used by permission.

Excerpt reprinted from *Self-Esteem: The New Reformation* by Robert Schuller, copyright 1982, Word Books, Waco, Texas 76796. Used by permission.

Excerpt from *What More Can God Say?* by Ray Stedman (second edition), copyright 1977, Regal Books, Ventura, California 93006. Used by permission.

Excerpt reprinted from *Whatever Became of Sin?* by Karl Menninger, M.D., copyright 1973, Dutton, New York, New York 10016. Used by permission.

Unless otherwise noted, all Scripture quotations are from the *New American Standard Bible,* copyright 1960, 1962, 1963, 1968, 1971, 1972, 1973, 1975, 1977 by The Lockman Foundation, or from the King James (Authorized) Version (KJV).

First printing, January 1987

*To my husband, Terry,
and to my parents, Dr. Karl and Laura Palmberg*

# CONTENTS

# ACKNOWLEDGMENTS

This book reflects my own journey to wholeness and is the result of many sources of positive input, the most significant of which I will mention in appreciation. Years ago at Westmont College, I derived much from my first formal attempts to integrate my Christian faith and the social sciences. Sometime thereafter in graduate school, several professors whose ideas can be found in this book greatly facilitated my integrative efforts. They included Dr. Donald F. Tweedie, Jr., formerly of Fuller Graduate School of Psychology, as well as the following who either were or are on the faculty of Rosemead School of Psychology: Dr. S. Bruce Narramore, Dr. William M. Counts, Dr. Maurice W. Wagner, and Dr. John D. Carter. All along the way, my parents, Dr. Karl and Laura Palmberg, have graciously supported and stimulated my efforts.

More currently, some of my clients and other individuals have contributed greatly by giving me permission to use their real life stories for the benefit of others. I am especially grateful to them.

Most of all, I thank my beloved husband, Dr. Terry R. Mathis, a philosopher who is himself a published author, who directly interacted with the ideas herein as the "first editor" of the manuscript. I am also indebted to Vicki deVries for her sensitivity and skill in further editing the manuscript for Tyndale.

While I am appreciative to all who influenced and supported the writing of this book, I of course am solely responsible for the views I have expressed. My desire is that they bring healing, freedom, wholeness, and joy to the reader.

# 1
# WHY DO I
# FEEL LIKE A NOBODY?

"Put the gun down!" I ordered Linda.

She was sitting at the personnel manager's desk on the third floor of a corporate office building. Her manager had fled after having put Linda on the phone with me.

"Linda, put it down right now!" I directed. "Live!"

"I have to cut you off," she replied. "Someone's on the other line, and I don't know how to use this phone."

There was the buzzing from the incoming call, a click, then silence.

Elsie, my secretary, scrambled to help me look up the phone number to call her back. Would the switchboard operator figure out which of all the hundreds of extensions to connect me with?

At last I got Linda and asked what happened.

"Some man called," she said. "He told me to do it – to pull the trigger."

"He's wrong, Linda. Don't do it!"

Nearly two hours passed as we wrestled over her life. I kept trying to find out why she was suicidal and continually urged her to put the gun down and live. Someone would repeatedly buzz the other line. As Linda would pick up the incoming call, her lifeline to me would be broken. The unknown caller would then dare her to "have the guts to pull the trigger." The switchboard operator became proficient at reconnecting me, but for some reason was not able to screen out the other caller.

"Linda, put the gun on the desk and walk out of the room.

11

No one will hurt you," I persisted. Even as I was speaking, Elsie was communicating with the SWAT team on our other line. Meanwhile, the building had been evacuated, and law enforcement officers and reporters were surrounding the building. Traffic at the busy intersection during the peak of holiday shopping was backed up for blocks. Inside, a human life hung by a thread.

"Put—the—gun—on—the—desk—and—walk—out!" I said, emphasizing every word.

Silence.

Was she dead? Or had she followed my directions and given herself up? I waited.

Elsie brought a message from the SWAT team. It read, "We have her."

She was alive!

Linda was a lovely, charming young woman with a problem that had almost taken her life. The problem? Low self-esteem.

While not everyone experiences low self-esteem to the life-threatening degree that Linda did, probably all of us have absorbed assaults on our personal value. Getting some bumps and bruises on our self-esteem is simply one of the occupational hazards of making our way through life.

Some might say that low self-esteem is not a serious complication, but low self-esteem is at least a contributing factor, if not the chief one, in most emotional problems. You may be surprised to learn of how many problems can result from, or be accompanied by, low self-esteem. The list is lengthy:

♦ Depression
♦ Anxiety
♦ Guilt or shame
♦ Fear of rejection
♦ Bitterness
♦ Indecision
♦ Living to please others

- Not knowing who I am
- Defensiveness or oversensitivity to criticism
- Stubbornness, rebellion, argumentativeness
- Shyness or withdrawal
- Alcohol or drug abuse
- Sexual promiscuity
- Habitual overworking
- Underachievement at school or work
- Bulimia (overeating) or anorexia (self-starvation)
- Greediness
- Fear of failure
- Lack of self-confidence
- Inability to communicate on a deep level
- Abusing others physically or verbally
- Suspicion, jealousy, or distrust
- Fear of expressing love or anger
- Lack of social skills
- Feeling of having nothing to offer for ministry to others
- Difficulty believing in God's love and acceptance

Most of us, myself included, experience some ways in which our self-esteem is less than what we wish it was. We also experience the destructive results. The end result of low self-esteem can be needless misery and lessened effectiveness in Christ's kingdom. Yet, healing our low self-esteem can enable us to live longer, healthier lives, enjoy greater personal happiness, and multiply our ministry and impact for Christ many times over. The dividends can be numerous and eternal.

It is helpful to understand how personal experiences can affect our self-image. Knowing the cause of a problem often makes it easier to solve the problem. This chapter explains some primary sources of low self-esteem, and the following chapters show how low self-esteem is healed. The bad news will be followed by the good news.

## Critical Tapes

"Why do I feel like a nobody?" "How did I develop low self-esteem?" Have you ever asked yourself questions like these?

Our first impressions about our worth come from what others directly or indirectly tell us as we are growing up. In childhood we are quite dependent on what other people think of us. Many people — parents, siblings, other relatives, friends, neighbors, teachers and classmates, pastors, Sunday school teachers, and numerous others — reveal their evaluations of our lovableness by the way they treat us. From day one, the most important people in our lives send us messages about our value. The more important the other person is, the more importance we give to the message received.

These messages become recordings in our minds, something like tape recordings, which are available for replay at any time as we go through life. How others talk to, behave toward, and feel about us affects how we think, feel, and speak about ourselves. The beliefs that important people in our childhood years hold about our value lay the foundation for the beliefs we develop about ourselves.

In this book, we will refer to recorded messages that were critical of us and that devalued us as "critical tapes." The persons who gave us critical tapes will be called "critical persons."[1]

Psychologists recognize at least three general areas contributing to the development of a healthy self-image: *feelings of belongingness, worthiness,* and *competence.* These are sometimes referred to as the "triad of self-esteem."

As three tones blend together to make one chord, so these three kinds of feelings integrate to form our self-concept. They overlap one another, yet we can describe them separately.[2] The attitudes of others impact upon these three areas of our self-esteem — for better or for worse.

## Do I Belong?

Belongingness is the sense of closeness with others that makes us feel wanted and secure. It is the deeply rooted conviction that the important people in our life want and include us. We are card-carrying members of the human race. We matter as much as anybody else. We belong.

As children, we begin to develop feelings of belongingness even in infancy. Normally, a close attachment develops between mother and child as the mother readily responds to her baby's signals of feelings and needs and expresses delight in interacting with her infant. Such responsiveness does not result in "spoiling" the infant. Instead, the more consistently the mother (or primary parent-figure) responds in these ways, the more her young child will evidence feelings of security, good self-esteem, confidence, and interest in exploring his or her world.[3]

Continued messages of belongingness are ordinarily given throughout childhood. Through personal attention and affection, parents and important others communicate, "I am delighted that you are mine. I'm so glad you're here. You are lovable no matter what. You belong."

This is the attitude that the Scriptures call *agape*, or unconditional, unchangeable love. It is love that does not have to be earned or merited. Value is bestowed with no strings attached. Jesus communicated this kind of love for children when he said, "Permit the children to come to Me; do not hinder them; for the kingdom of God belongs to such as these" (Mark 10:14b).

## What Makes Us Feel Left Out

Five things can make a person feel that he or she does not belong: rejection, neglect, ridicule, threat of abandonment, and favoritism.

*Rejection.* Rejection comes in several forms. In general, people feel rejected when they receive messages, either overt or subtle, that their existence is resented. A woman who grew up in a Christian home told me, "I know now that I was an abused child. Every morning Mother threw me out the front door, saying, 'Don't come back. I don't want you!' Crying all the way to school, I felt so hollow that I thought my lungs would collapse. That was how I often began a school day."

As a girl, she was often beaten for no apparent reason and wondered if her teachers ever questioned why she frequently had bruises. Since her father was on the school board, perhaps they felt awkward asking questions.

Physical abuse is, of course, an extreme form of rejection. More typical is verbal abuse. A mother may tell her daughter, "If it weren't for you, I could have had a career," or a financially troubled father may tell his children, "If it weren't for you, I'd be a lot better off financially." These parents are guilty of verbal rejection. Such parents are expressing resentment that their children exist: "My world would be a better place if you were not here. You are an imposition on my life, an unwanted interruption."

While it is normal for a parent to experience these feelings at times, conveying them to a child can be harmful, if not devastating. Extreme or repeated parental rejection may become recorded by the child's mind as a critical tape and can contribute to a self-critical attitude the child adopts. The child may come to think, *Other people would be better off if I disappeared from the earth. They can bother me with their needs, but I should not ask them to help me with mine. I don't matter as others do. I don't belong.*

*Neglect.* Another way of conveying to a child that he or she does not belong is less direct than rejection. Its name is neglect. Here the child gets *inadequate attention.*

The ultimate form of neglect would be when the child is left in the crib and touched only when absolutely necessary to maintain his or her physical survival. In a case like this, the child may live only a few months, because he or she has been deprived of the affection needed to endure physically as well as emotionally.

Neglect also comes in other more common forms. One young woman recalls that in her childhood her parents paid a lot of attention to the children, but always on a group basis. The whole family would go to church, swim at the beach, ride the merry-go-round at an amusement park, or dine at a family restaurant. She does not recall ever receiving one-on-one attention from either of her parents. True, they cared for her, but she did not feel a special sense of belonging to them, of being tied to either parent as one person to another.

*What mysterious thing must be wrong with me?* she wondered. *Why did my parents seem not to want to be with me just for myself? Am I uninteresting or unlovable?*

As a by-product of her feelings of neglect, she had trouble feeling close to her parents or to anyone else. As an adult, she came to faith in Christ but had difficulty feeling she belonged closely to him. She believed in Jesus, but could not experience a sense of intimacy, of personal one-on-one attachment with him. Neglect had taken not only its psychological toll, but its spiritual one as well.

*Ridicule.* Janice eyed her new baby sister, Theresa, as unwanted competition for her parents' love. Her goal was to make sure Theresa always knew her place. Her strategy? Ridicule, the third cause behind a lack of belongingness.

Janice teased Theresa about the clothes she wore, the dolls she liked to play with—everything. Theresa believed she must be an inadequate person, because everything about her was ridiculed. She shied away from making friends, expecting that people would be just like her sister, Janice, ridiculing her and not letting her belong with them. Here Theresa got attention, but it was negative.

*Threat of Abandonment.* A very direct way to communicate to a child that he or she does not belong is through threat of abandonment.

One blazingly hot day, I was in a park and saw a toddler trying very hard to get a drink from a water fountain. His mother thought it was time to go, however. Expressing impatience with him, she said, "If you don't come right now, I'm

17

going to leave you." She turned on her heel and walked briskly toward the exit. The boy ran crying after her as fast as his little legs would carry him. Evidently, he really believed she would abandon him, and so his sense of belonging was dependent on whether he towed her line and did it quickly.

A girl whose adoptive mother often told her, "If you don't do what we say, we can send you back," experienced similar feelings. Later as an adult, she believed that if she displeased her husband, he would leave her, too. She lived in fear of abandonment, thinking she must have some basic, mysterious defect that caused people not to want her.

*Favoritism.* A fifth way a child may come to feel he or she does not belong is by a parent systematically showing preference to one child. Sometimes the favoritism is actual, other times only perceived.

Janie always knew her mother loved her, but she never felt she had as close an attachment to her mother as her brother did. For example, she explained, "Neither of us was supposed to tattle on the other. If he'd tell on me, I'd get in trouble. But if I'd tell on him, I'd get scolded for being a 'tattle-tale.'

"As for how we were punished, he never got whipped—only reprimanded. I always got whipped with a hanger or a belt. One time when we were playing together, he slammed a door in my face and I got cut under my eye. In turn, I hurt his arm. Mom made a fuss over his arm and paid little attention to my cut. In fact, she accused me of having provoked him to do it.

"When it came to giving us attention, Mom always had time to go to his sports events, which were after her work. She never felt obligated to take time off work to go to mine, which were just as important to me. She seemed to like having little boys around and going to their activities. I was confused about whether she liked me as a girl.

"I'm sure if I told her someday how I felt, she'd understand, but I can't talk to her. I just want to feel special and lovable to her."

Another victim of long-term partiality was the middle child of a family of three daughters. The older and younger sisters always played together and left her out. Now an adult, the "middle child" still struggles with the feeling that when she is in a group of people, she will be left out. Her critical tape says, "You don't belong."

Rejection, neglect, ridicule, threat of abandonment, or favoritism—each of these can make a child or an adult feel he does not belong.

Belongingness, as the first area of self-esteem that comes into play, is shaped in our infancy, but we continue to get messages about it all our lives. By and large, parents accept infants as they are just because they exist. We do not place many expectations on them. Even though we expect older children and adults to fulfill responsibilities, ideally, there still should be a similar kind of unconditional acceptance granted among adults.

An adequate sense of belongingness paves the way for developing feelings of worthiness, the second part of the self-esteem triad. After the question "Do I belong?" comes another most important one: "Do I deserve love?"

## Am I Worthy of Love?

When children near the end of the first year of life and begin the second year, parents start to expect them to learn what is acceptable and what isn't. Loving, not harsh, discipline is crucial to keeping the child's sense of being worthy of love intact and undamaged. Otherwise, he may become discouraged and internalize a critical tape that says, "When I do wrong, I am a terrible person and no longer deserving of love." He may develop a feeling of worthlessness, the opposite of what the second crucial part of the self-esteem triad requires.

The Scriptures admonish parents in Colossians 3:21: "Do not exasperate your children, that they may not lose heart." Following this advice can help parents teach their children and enable their children to feel worthwhile at the same time.

## What Makes Us Feel Worthless?

The danger factors contributing to feelings of worthlessness include hostile discipline, permissiveness, inconsistency, and overcontrol.

*Hostile Discipline.* One of the most obvious ways to make a child feel worthless when he does wrong is through hostile discipline. I personally observed the following scene in a grocery store.

Two boys were toying with a jar of honey and inevitably dropped it. The glass jar shattered, smearing honey all over the floor. Then their mother went into action. She tensed her muscles, hardened her face, and erupted like an angry volcano.

She scared me, and I was her size! Imagine how she must have looked to her boys, who were half her size. They each must have felt terrified and despised, concluding that "when I do something wrong, I am trash, and something frightening is going to happen."

One woman shared an extreme case of hostile discipline with me. In her early childhood, she had been cruelly punished for such minor misbehavior as accidentally leaving her little fingerprints on a window. Discipline often came in the form of being forced to overdose on laxatives or to drink Tabasco sauce. If a bus passed her house, her mother would say, "Do you see that bus? It takes bad little girls to the mental hospital. If you're bad, we'll put you on that bus, and if you tell them you don't belong on it, they won't believe you."

That little girl grew up to be a woman who lacked feelings of self-worth and belongingness to such an extent that she even expressed doubt about being a member of the human race. Convinced that she could not understand, or be understood by, a human being, she wanted to get counseling from a computer that could answer her questions. Clearly, she was a victim of severe hostile discipline.

*Permissiveness.* The opposite of hostile discipline is permissiveness, and this, too, can lead a child to feel worthless. Picture a little girl sitting on the front seat of her car, riding home with her mother. Reaching into the grocery bag, the girl takes out a chocolate bar, and her mother says, "Lucy, don't eat that candy bar. It will ruin your appetite for dinner." Lucy unwraps the candy and takes her first bite. Her mother yells, "Lucy, I told you, 'Don't eat that candy bar.' "

Lucy takes another bite. "Lucy, stop!" her mother scolds. The girl ignores the order and finishes the candy bar. Her mother screams, "I told you not to eat that candy bar!"

Lucy knows that eating the candy bar is wrong. That is, she physically hears that message, but without a follow-through of parental discipline, she does not learn self-discipline.

As a young adult, Lucy will frequently replay to herself the critical tape convictions she learned as a girl. "I'm just a bad person. I can't stop. I always do wrong things. I know they're wrong, yet I still do them. I have no brakes. I guess I was just born rotten." A childhood without loving, firm, consistent enforcement of guidelines paves the way for an adulthood of self-fulfilling anarchy.

*Inconsistency.* A third contributor to a sense of worthlessness is the practice of switch-hitting between the two extremes of severe discipline and permissiveness—inconsistent discipline. In one situation, the mother would either verbally devour or ignore her son when he disobeyed, depending on her mood. When his father or a schoolteacher got after him, the mother sometimes acted as though her "little angel" could do no wrong. The boy was confused.

Since the rules kept changing on him, he could not predict and influence whether he would get approval or disapproval. He expressed his self-image as a feeling that he was a helpless, powerless person, just as though he had no arms or legs. His feelings of self-worth seemed to fluctuate unpredictably, and he felt helpless in coping with her inconsistency in both discipline and emotional support.

With both dependable loving discipline and consistent loving support, children will have an easier time learning appropriate guidelines for their behavior, as well as internalizing a stable, positive self-image.

*Overcontrol.* Sometimes instead of disciplining children for wrong or harmful behavior, parents punish them for normal attempts to develop their own separate personalities. Some parents may feel anxious when their toddler begins to develop rudimentary skills toward independence such as walking or saying no. They may feel, "Now she doesn't need me," or "He'll pass me up in confidence and self-esteem," or "She's rejecting me."

Children can sense when a parent is withdrawing emotional support or even attacking critically. In this case, the child may grow up fearing, "If I express or act on my own judgment and feelings, I will be abandoned and left helpless. I better work hard to please others, even at the expense of not being me." Such a child often feels dominated and dependent. As depressing, angering, and guilt-inducing as this dependent way of relating is, it may become the only way by which this individual can feel close and secure. Unfortunately, this person will likely feel emotionally inadequate and unworthy of someone who relates in a more wholesome way.

While longing for a more genuine and mature type of closeness, this individual will likely also protect himself or herself from it (whether knowingly or unknowingly). Why? Because to be close in a nonclingy way, a person has to allow himself or herself to become a separate, independent, fully functioning self. And the fear of being emotionally abandoned for trying to become a self is great.

One person who gave in to parental domination described to me her deep feelings of worthlessness and loss of personhood. She wrote:

> I realize I was brought up to be the person others wanted me to be so that they would like me and not be bothered by my presence.
>
> But their molding process failed. That person was not me. By the time they were finished with their futile effort, I was left scattered and in pieces.
>
> In many ways I am still in pieces. Even with help it's hard to glue together fragments of myself and make them into a whole person. I feel like there was just too much damage done long ago and that even now there is something broken in the works beyond repair.
>
> I don't really like myself. I never have. In many ways, I'm not what I seem or what I appear to be. In truth I'm two people. And I struggle to control the dark side of my nature, lest it give me away.
>
> I'm a wearer of masks and a player of parts. And I always live in fear that I'll be found out one day. No one can live a lie forever.
>
> I hate myself for what I am, but even more so for what I'm not — a person.[4]

This woman's deep feelings of worthlessness are obvious. Parental domination has led to self-hostility and the attempt to give up her personhood, but, of course, she cannot — even in death — because her unique self is real and eternal.

The other typical way of reacting to overcontrol is rebellion. Jim's father lectured him mercilessly about his personal tastes, clothes, hairstyle, friends, hobbies, homework, and future vocation — all "for his own good." Resenting that conditions were placed on his worth, Jim rebelled and decided to be the opposite of everything his father wanted him to be.

Jim, like many rebels, tried to numb his depression and anger by diverting his attention to self-destructive behavior such as alcohol abuse, immorality, excessive pleasure-seeking, and dangerous recreational activities. Conflict with teachers, employers, and his own wife and children became his pattern. The only positive aspect was that he did not allow his personhood to be crushed entirely. "I feel like a blade of grass pushing up through a crack in a concrete slab," he commented.

One form of overdomination that deserves special attention in its own right is disallowing feelings. Trying to discipline a child for feelings, rather than for behavior, is an example of extreme personality control.

June's mother was fearful of anger. Having been disciplined in anger as a child, she now felt she had to accept anger from her husband, but she was not going to take it from her daughter, June. As a result, June was not allowed to feel anger toward her mother—at least, not to show it in any way. Ironically, June was disciplined in anger when she showed anger. She came to believe her critical tape, "If I feel anger, I am a bad, terrible, unlovable person."

Had her mother taught June how to handle anger in an honest, constructive way, June could have learned to cope with feelings of anger, as well as to develop a sense of self-worth.

When June became a mother, she in turn began to play back the "repressed anger" tape to guide her actions toward her own children. Still, she had enough self-awareness to be concerned about this and wanted to change.

Feelings of worthlessness can spring from hostile discipline, permissiveness, inconsistency, and overcontrol. The way we were disciplined is recorded in our own thoughts and feelings and shapes our values about what we should be and whether we are still lovable when we fall short.

Feelings of belongingness and worthiness are the first two parts of the self-esteem triad. However, as important as they are in the development of self-esteem, they require a third partner: feelings of competence.

**Am I Competent?**
The third area of self-esteem is reflected in the statement: "I am capable of doing things for myself, and my capabilities are good enough. I have some abilities that are very rewarding to me. I can take charge of my own responsibilities."

Researchers ran an experiment in which they trained some of the students in a nursery school class to put on their coats. At the end of day, the teacher offered to help both the trained and untrained children put on their coats. The researchers noticed that the ones who knew how to put on their own coats *chose* to do so for themselves.[5] They *wanted to.*

Who can disagree that it feels good to be able to do something for yourself under your own power? Competence is its own reward,[6] and adults normally encourage it in children. Parents usually help their children become capable so that when they reach adulthood, they will be ready to go out on their own.

The Scriptures praise competence as a worthy value to pursue. Proverbs 22:29 says, "Do you see a man skilled in his work? He will stand before kings; He will not stand before obscure men." God wants us to experience the joy and satisfaction of developing the unique capabilities with which he has gifted us.

**What Hinders Our Sense of Competence?**
Some conditions hinder the normal development of a child's feelings of competence. Encouragement of overdependence, overprotection, lack of praise, and perfectionism are critical messages that can alter the course of a child's journey into self-esteem.

*Overdependence.* One situation illustrates the damage done by overdependence. Penny's mother lacked a meaningful friendship with anyone except her daughter. She was emotionally dependent on Penny and wanted to keep her around. One way to do that was to keep Penny totally dependent on her. She did everything for her daughter including buttoning her buttons and tying her shoes far beyond the time when Penny was capable of doing these things for herself.

When Penny grew up, married, and had children, her husband could not tolerate her dependency on her mother. He left Penny because "Mother" was doing all their laundry, cooking all their meals, having them all sleep at her house, and generally dominating the family by keeping them dependent on her in every way possible. Penny, who was not developing her own separate, unique personality, lacked feelings of both worthiness and competence.

To Penny, becoming competent meant sacrificing some things—all those "favors" that were being done for her. As a step toward her autonomy, she redecorated her bedroom, selecting and paying for the furnishings rather than letting her mother head the project "as usual." Penny hung the wallpaper and sewed the curtains and bedspread herself, thus experiencing an exhilarating sense of satisfaction. Here was a healthy case of "Please, Mother. I'd rather do it myself!"

*Overprotection.* A retired man and active church member confided to me that his parents had overprotected him in his childhood, sheltering him in many ways. For example, he always had to bring his friends to *his* house; he could never go to theirs. When he had to give a speech in class at school, his parents would say, "Oh, Hank! You don't want to do that! They'll laugh at you!" Finally, when he reached adolescence, he realized something was wrong. Overprotection had not been building his confidence.

Hank wanted to go out for football to develop some competence, but of course that terrified his parents because it was "dangerous." As a result, he went out for football without their knowing it. Hank managed to play the whole season and win some awards before his parents ever found out—

which was quite an accomplishment given the pattern in his family. In the end, he told his parents what he had done in order to invite them to the awards banquet. However, they refused to attend with the excuse, "It's in front of all those people!"

Hank's parents felt most secure when surrounded by their family in the protective cocoon of their home. They attempted to keep Hank there, too, for "his" safety and thus prevented him from spreading wings and taking risks in the big world.

Overprotection is a problem with which I personally identify. Growing up, I felt I was a breakable person who could not competently take care of herself in the adult world. I had no idea why I felt this way until my mother one day shared with me that she and my father had handled me with "kid gloves" ever since I was born. They had supposed that their baby girl, the first daughter after two sons, would be more fragile than their sons had been. My mother also admitted that she had been struggling with low self-esteem as a woman at that time. Her lack of confidence in certain areas may have also affected the way she parented me.

I was grateful for her openness. Though I already loved her, this disclosure helped me love her even more. It also helped me "put the label on the can." I knew the critical tape with which I wrestled.

God, of course, did his part. In his mercy, he allowed some of my most catastrophic fantasies to come true. I survived! What a relief to experience that I was not as helpless as I had imagined. My feelings of competence rose when I discovered I did not need to be overprotected.

*Lack of Praise.* Lack of praise will also lead to decreased feelings of competence.

One day, Bill dutifully brought home a report card of all A's and one B. His father glanced up from the newspaper long enough to ask, "Why did you get the B?" He made no comment about all those *A*'s, only about the *B*.

This was a classic example to Bill of his parents' pattern. When he did anything poorly, his parents gave him attention and made a comment. When he did something well, his parents were relieved but said little. He came to respond similarly to himself: When he did something poorly, he verbally bloodied himself; when he did something well, he took it for granted, thinking, *That's just what I'm supposed to do.*

Living by his critical tapes, he gave himself no credit, no pats on the back, no feelings of competence. The effect of lack of praise was a lopsided self-image.

*Perfectionism.* Another competence-inhibitor is the all-too-common emphasis on perfection.

Walter remembers that as a boy he liked to make model airplanes—at first, that is. His father always found a way that it could have been "better," and Walter had to correct any imperfections. Unfortunately, Walter went through life looking upon everything as a somber chore, and he seldom had any fun. Even though he was competent in many ways, he did not consider himself competent. He could not decide how good was good enough.

Obviously, almost anything we've ever done could have been done better. We could have stayed up all day and all night, performing the particular task with microscopic perfection. However, if the standard for competency is doing the best that can possibly be attained, we may never reach it. In that case, we will never feel competent. Besides, some things do not deserve or require all that much effort and perfection.

Overdependence, overprotection, lack of praise, and perfectionism may stifle a child's sense of competence. When feelings of competence are lacking, a child's self-esteem will be less than wholesome. If a sense of belongingness and worthiness, the first two parts of the self-esteem triad, are also missing, it is inevitable that low self-esteem will be the devastating, long-term result.

## Summing It Up

The critical messages a person receives and records during childhood can affect him or her for life. Most people have some areas of their lives in which their self-esteem seems less than satisfactory. Despite the damage done to one's self-esteem, however, a person can find healing.

One of the first steps toward restoration must begin with self-exploration through which self-understanding can begin. The following exercises can help you begin that process. These exercises will not provide instant change, but they can certainly facilitate the healing process.

If you are recalling ways that you received critical messages about your belongingness, worthiness, or competence, keep these three basic components of self-esteem in mind as you read the chapters that follow. Your self-awareness will help you apply healing insights in more personalized, specific ways.

## Target Questions

1. Find a quiet, secluded place and relax for a few moments. Then mentally review the various causes of low self-esteem covered in this chapter. Which ones apply to yourself? Now pray about each area in which you would like God to help you have a more settled sense of your own worth.

2. This chapter presents the concept that we receive many messages, whether spoken or unspoken, from other people as we grow up. Remembering some of these messages may help us understand this concept.

For a fairly simple example, what did you learn at home about eating dessert? Did you learn it was the best part of the meal? That it was a reward you earned by eating the rest of your meal first? That dessert should be avoided because of calories? That it was for special occasions only?

Now remember what values you learned about music. What sorts of music were acceptable or unacceptable? How big a part of life did you learn that music should have?

What values did you learn about having fun? Education? Careers? Money? Marriage? Having children? Having friends? Going to church? Having a relationship with God?

Finally, with respect to your self-esteem, what did you learn about whether you belong? Do you feel worthwhile in comparison to most people? In comparison to God's standard of moral perfection? Do you feel worthy of love even when you do something wrong? Do you feel competent?

3. Think about someone you know who has a low self-image and how that self-image affects his life. Questions to guide your thinking could include:

    A.  Is he shy or afraid to make friends?

    B.  Is it difficult for him to make decisions?

    C.  Is it difficult for him to attempt various projects?

After reflecting on the topic, share your insights with someone you feel close to. Brainstorm together on how low self-esteem affects the way a person lives. Jot down these ideas and keep them for future reference. If you're studying with a group, list these ideas on a blackboard, if possible.

Meditate on these brainstorming ideas. Do you personally identify with any of them? On a piece of paper, list those items of personal concern. Ask God to give you the insights and power needed to change areas of weakness/defeat into areas of strength/victory.

## 2
# HOW DO I FORGIVE
# CRITICAL PEOPLE?

Jerry could never forget a conversation he had overheard between his parents years ago. As a boy, he had eavesdropped on his father, who had said, "I never wanted him in the first place." Jerry believed he was the person to whom his father was referring.

As Jerry was recounting this story, his wife and children were seated around him in my office. His young sons had become fidgety and were poking each other. This annoyed Jerry, who snarled in front of everyone, "I never wanted them anyway." I responded by asking him if he believed feeling unwanted himself had any bearing on his having said he did not want his own sons.

"That has nothing to do with it!" he snapped. "They are two entirely different situations."

Jerry had shown insight into the content of the critical messages he had received and into the identity of the critical persons. However, that was as far as he had gotten. Consequently, his insight merely served to make him bitter, and his bitterness kept him emotionally focused on his critical tapes. Furthermore, his resentment condemned him to reproduce his critical tapes in yet another generation of his family. He became ten times worse than his own critical person.

It is not enough to understand *how* we arrived at low self-esteem. We must go on to do something about it.

Perhaps you saw yourself in the last chapter — either as the child who was injured or as the parent who made mistakes.

Painful feelings or memories may have surfaced. If so, you are probably wondering what you can do about it now.

This chapter begins to chart the road to wholeness that will release you from the power of negative memories. It describes how to forgive your critical persons so that you can stop listening to your critical tapes and replace them with loving and affirming ones. But first, in case you read the last chapter as a parent, I want to offer some comfort.

## What If I Was the Critical Person?

If you are a parent, you may have identified with some of the mistakes described in chapter 1 and thought, *I flunked as a parent.* Raising the awareness of parents is bound to elevate their guilt feelings as well. There is ample temptation to become a critical person to yourself for having been a critical parent.

You may be wondering, *What do I do after I've already blundered?* First and foremost, you should forgive yourself. After all, there is no perfect parent except our heavenly Father. Humanly speaking, imperfect parents are the only kind there is.

But what can we do about our blunders? The most valuable thing a parent can do after he or she has been harmful is to admit it to the child and, if the child is not already aware of it, explain what the parent did wrong. Even if your child is grown, it can be helpful to explain to him or her, "I think I was off target and may have hurt you. You may have had some feelings that something was wrong, and now I want to spell out what I did, because it might help you." The following story is an example of a mother who did this.

A young woman was suddenly widowed after the birth of her first child, a boy who had serious medical problems for years. Fearful that if he died she would be unable to bear the loss of all she held dear in the world, she did not allow herself to become too emotionally attached to him. She was sure she came across as rejecting him, even though she loved him very much.

This son, a very intelligent boy, took an interest in science and computer games, but he was a loner. He never opened up to anyone. His mother realized that he needed to be close to people and she was missing the enjoyment of contact with her son. Since she had not given him much emotional support, she was concerned that he might take the blame and think himself unlovable.

One day she decided to try to explain the problem to him. At home, casually she told him how she had been afraid of getting too close when he was so ill because she was afraid of losing him. She said that she had feared she would not be able to bear that loss. She said it was not his fault she had not spent time with him, and she hoped they now would be able to talk about more things together.

When she said this, her son listened but showed no response and want back to playing. She wondered whether what she had said had done any good.

Over the next several days, she noticed that when she asked a question such as, "How was school today?" he would give a longer answer than usual. Sometimes he would stop by the kitchen while she prepared dinner and voluntarily talk about his interests and activities. They were getting closer. He seemed to feel more that he belonged. As she got to know him better, she marvelled, "He's such an interesting person! I like him!"

A parent's admitting mistakes to a child can be a pivotal turning point in undoing the effects of critical messages. Even when a child has already grown to adulthood, explaining parental mistakes can be healing.

Turning the table, should adults confront their parents about their parenting mistakes? One of my clients reported, "I told my parents it was their fault that my sister and I have emotional problems. They said that was absolutely untrue."

Although I suggest that parents admit their errors to their children, I do *not* urge grown children to go back to their parents with a list of all the wrongs their parents perpetrated against them. Usually the motive for unloading on a parent in this way is either (1) to get closure and freedom finally by having the parent admit mistakes or (2) to get revenge.

The first motive is, generally speaking, unrealistic. Most people, parents included, will simply defend themselves against a recitation of all their faults. If you have open, relatively undefensive parents, perhaps a very tactful presentation will work. You might bring up one of your least sensitive items as a trial balloon. If you get only a defensive response, let it go. You may have to talk through your complaints with someone else.

If, on the other hand, your motive is to machine-gun them with all their sins and get revenge, forget it. That is not fair to your parents (or whoever your critical persons are) and will not heal them. Instead, vent your anger to someone else, such as a good friend, pastor, or counselor who can help you resolve it.

## Understanding the Critical Persons
We have already begun to address how a self-image can be healed. Now we need to find out how to let go of our critical tapes and their power over us. The first and single most important means to accomplishing this goal is forgiving the critical person whose message we recorded and keep replaying. Bitterness and resentment will keep us emotionally focused on our critical tapes, whereas forgiveness will help give us emotional release.

Understanding our critical persons is crucial in this release. Why were people critical of our worth? More than likely, it was because they had the same problem. They had had critical persons, too. Consequently, they too did not understand what gave them worth, and they could pass on only as much affirmation of worthiness as they themselves understood. Ellen was a case in point.

Trying to repair the relationship, Ellen invited her young adult daughter for a prolonged stay at her house. During the visit one evening, she had to have her daughter pick her up from work. When her daughter arrived in an old family car,

Ellen felt humiliated to be seen in it by her fellow employees. Instead of proudly introducing her daughter, she hurried into the sedan and scolded her daughter for arriving in that particular car.

"I was busy listening to my critical tapes that said, 'What will people think?' " Ellen recalled. "I completely forgot what a favor my daughter was doing to pick me up at all. I never thanked her. That's exactly the kind of thing my mother used to do to me."

Ellen believed her personal worth depended on making the right impression. What she had inherited from her mother, Ellen had bequeathed to her own daughter.

Most people are democratic — they are as critical of others as they are of themselves. That is probably why whoever was to blame — our parents, siblings, friends, neighbors, employers — mistreated us. No wonder they infected us with their disease. They could not love us unconditionally any better than they could love themselves unconditionally.

## We Had Our Own Point of View

Let's face it — we as children probably did not love our parents unconditionally either. We were less-than-perfect children interacting with less-than-perfect parents and other people. Sin has affected us all. Our own fallenness as children has influenced even our interpretation of the messages handed to us, as the following account illustrates.

"Willy is your favorite!" Bobby would accuse. Although knowing from experience she was wasting her breath, his mother, Mary Ann, would try again to reassure Bobby. Willy had always been a sickly child who needed considerable care from his mother. Also, academic learning came slowly for him, and he needed more tutoring from his mother.

Bobby on the other hand, was certain the extra attention meant his mother loved Willy more. Actually, Bobby was a very active and adventurous child who required more discipline, which he interpreted as evidence of his mother's personal disliking.

35

Mary Ann confided to me, "I like Bobby better because I admire his abilities and assertiveness. I've always been a timid person. But when I tell him how proud I am of his good grades and leadership in Boy Scouts, he braggingly uses it to put down Willy. Then I'm afraid to praise Bobby for anything. All the cards are stacked against Bobby. He reads me his own way."

Even if we had had perfect parents, we would not necessarily have been able to perceive them accurately, because we were not perfect children. It is not merely the actual behavior of others that affects us; it is how we perceive their behavior, too.

## Admit They Were Wrong

Where others have indeed hurt us, even though we may understand why they did it, we need to admit that they were wrong and that there was something for which to forgive them. The other alternative is to agree with them and say, "It's all true. I am a reject. I have no value."

One man confessed what a battle it was for him to face the fact that important people in his life were wrong, because he had always respected them so much. Sometimes we do not like to admit others have made mistakes, but that is reality, the hazard of growing up in a very human world.

Whether it is easy to admit or not, most of us have felt angry when we've been hurt. Surprisingly, that emotional response may tell us something useful. When you were put down, did you resent it? If so, that was because part of you knows that the put-down was wrong, that you have worth, and that you should have been treated with love. Build self-affirmation, not bitterness, on that bedrock conviction.

## Forgiveness Is Freedom

The next step after understanding our critical persons is to forgive them. Forgiveness takes a lot of the sting and power out of those unloving messages. By holding grudges, we carry the burden of the tapes a lot longer, and it is much harder to stop listening to them. We cannot be emotionally charged about something and emotionally released from it at the same time. When I let go of my punishing resentment against my critical person, I disconnect myself from my emotional attachment to his critical message.

By forgiveness, I do not mean we should do as one man who called his dad long distance to tell him, "I forgive you for all the things you did to me." His father hung up on him. It had never occurred to the father that he needed such forgiveness. He felt insulted. Oftentimes, forgiveness needs to be limited to a change of inner attitude that is not so directly expressed.

## Forgiveness as a Goal
People are not instantly able to forgive just because they know they should.

"All my life I have struggled," a woman told me, "to forgive my mother for not wanting me. People keep quoting verses at me. I guess they do that in case I didn't know it was wrong that I haven't forgiven. Each time I only feel more guilty but still don't know how to get over my bitterness and forgive her. I don't need more sermonizing—I need a brass-tacks answer!"

Being able to forgive may mean knowing this: forgiveness is like a goal attained at the end of a process. In my counseling experience, I have observed that forgiving critical persons usually does not occur in a single momentous or emotionally dramatic event. Most commonly, it is a *gradual* change that occurs as an individual comes to understand the critical persons' own low self-esteem. Empathy is involved here as a person lets go of the grudges or hostility he has been harboring against the critical person.

## Forgiving Parents
If the critical persons were our parents, it may help to remember that few parents have courses in parenting. Nor do I think a parent sits down and premeditates, *How can I damage*

*my child's self-image today?* Parents just parent the way they know how, and that is all they can do. We have to give them permission to have faults and make mistakes.

We may discover we have a double standard for authority figures such as parents. We may be expecting that a person in authority is supposed to be perfect and never let us down. If so, we may need to take our superheros or supervillains off the pedestal and allow them to be card-carrying members of the human race.

I used to think there were three types of people: males, females, and authority figures. When it finally dawned on me that authority figures are people – no better, no worse – I stopped being so crushed when, of all things, they acted like human beings.

## Forgiving the Unrepentant

"But," you may be asking, "what if my critical persons are my parents, and they are not asking to be forgiven? They think they did a great job. If I turned out badly, it is all my fault. I am just all messed up. They are putting all the blame on me." In other words, they are not about to make it easy for you to forgive them. Instead, they make you even angrier.

A young woman who faced this problem complained that her mother had belittled her for having emotional problems, implying that she herself was a rather ideal mother. The daughter asked her mother, "Do you believe you have any faults?" Her mother agreed in principle that she had. However, when the daughter asked her mother to name one, she could not think of any.

The daughter saw her mother as the impenetrable Great Wall of China, and herself as a badly splintered battering ram. What she did not see was that behind that stubbornly self-righteous exterior, her mother was more like an easily crushed China doll. When this daughter saw the truth and felt compassion for her mother's brokenness, she forgave her mother for being too damaged to provide the openness and caring for which she hungered.

It is hard to forgive a parent with a defensive attitude. However, it is painful for parents to think that they have harmed their own children. Parents may suppose their worth partly depends on how well they performed as parents. If so, they are trying to earn their worthiness, instead of accepting it from God as a given. Furthermore, most parents love their children and do not want to think they have hurt them.

Sometimes people are afraid to forgive an unrepentant critical person, because they believe that to forgive is to forget. Yet they may be well aware that the person they need to forgive has not changed, shows no inclination toward ever changing, and in all probability will continue to be hurtful.

I do not think forgiving means nobly denying what this critical person is like. "Forgive and forget" can result in your becoming mincemeat. Instead, forgiving means no longer harboring resentment as a form of revenge against this person for his or her sins.

## God's Justice

It is hard to forgive someone who goes on hurting you and does not repent. One time the only way I could forgive some critical persons who were not at all likely to change was to leave the responsibility for dishing out justice in God's hands, not mine. Ironically, what helped was God's promise, "Vengeance is mine. I will repay" (Romans 12:19).

I decided that if I tried to get even with them, I would do it in a way that would destroy; but God would do it in a constructive way that would give them an opportunity to repent and change. Besides, I felt so hurt at the time that there was nothing I could have done to my critical persons that would have felt adequate to express my rage or to punish them. Revenge would not have satisfied. My resentment was eating me up and only making me miserably unhappy.

By faith, I gave the responsibility of justice to God (and kept giving it to him again each time I felt rage toward these persons). I did not indulge in fantasies of God giving them their due (Proverbs 24:17-18). Instead, I trusted him to be just and loving to them and surrendered my miserable avenger role entirely. What a load off my back!

By no longer focusing on my rage against them, I was freed to see the other persons in a more open-minded and realistic way. I began to understand from their point of view why they had behaved as they had, even though I still believed their behavior had been wrong, and I then was able to start forgiving them from my heart. The critical tape I received from them began losing its power over me.

Experiencing even more emotional freedom from the influence of their message, I discovered a part of myself, a critical tape, that put me down in a way similar to the way they had. They were not my sole problem. When I corrected my perception of myself, I was truly free of that self-esteem problem and of the resentment that had robbed my happiness. I began to love them and myself in a new way. Turning over to God my need for justice became my means to forgiveness and healing.

## I Am a Critical Person

Another way to forgive critical persons is to remember that "I am one, too." We may do well to consider the question, "Have I been a critical person toward the critical persons in my life? I feel they did not love me despite my faults. Do I love them despite their faults?"

Jesus said, "Condemn not, lest you be condemned yourselves" (Matthew 7:1, my translation). If we point an accusing finger at others, we aim it at ourselves as well. We have to be forgiven by Christ for having done the same sorts of unloving things that others have done to us. That is why Paul said in Ephesians 4:32, "And be kind to one another, tenderhearted, forgiving each other, just as God in Christ also has forgiven you."

I learned this principle from a former employer of mine who seemed to relish making my life miserable. Although we were both Christians, I distinctly felt he was trying to label me with a particular brand of spirituality that he rejected. For months, unrelentingly, he had nothing positive to say about me unless he discounted it in the next breath. I became increasingly resentful and on several occasions confronted him, not always with the best attitude. He seemed to hear me, but he never changed. Finally he confronted *me*. "You need to be forgiven, too, because you have rejected me also." He was right. I asked his forgiveness.

All of us have been someone's critical person at one time or another. If we condemn others for unloving acts, we condemn ourselves as well.

About a dozen years ago, Thomas Harris captured the attitude of peace with oneself and others in the phrase that served as the title of his popular book *I'm OK — You're OK*.[1] Subsequently, Newton Malony, a professor at Fuller Theological Seminary, seeking to emphasize the Christian understanding of forgiveness through grace, rephrased the ideal attitude this way: "I'm not OK — you're not OK, and that's OK."[2]

"For all have sinned," the Scriptures say (Romans 3:23). We have failed to love our neighbors as ourselves (Matthew 22:36-40). Each and every one of us has been a critical person, but God loves and forgives sinners, even critical persons. He calls us to do likewise, and thus, to change from being critical persons to gracious lovers.

## Summing It Up

His forgiveness releases us from the penalty for being critical persons. While forgiveness may be a process, we can progress toward our goal by understanding our critical persons, letting them have faults, too, and letting God take care of our need for justice. In turn, by asking others to forgive us, we are helping them to let go of the hurt our critical messages toward them have caused. Our forgiveness saves us from enslavement to our critical tapes. *Forgiveness is the power to change the past, present, and future impact of critical persons.*

Forgiving our critical persons enables us to stop brooding

41

about our critical tapes so we can then replace them with affirming tapes. The next chapter describes this process of replacement.

## Target Questions

1. If you are a parent, are there some mistakes you made that concern you now? How would you feel about admitting your mistake(s) to your child? If you wish to tell your child, how would you want to phrase it?

2. Did your parents ever admit mistakes to you? How did you feel about it? Did it help (or would it have helped)?

3. Who are your critical persons? Why do you think they hurt you as they did? How adequate were their self-images?

4. Is there someone you have not yet forgiven? What is stopping you? (Mark all that apply.)

    A. I have been waiting for that person to admit to being wrong, and it has not happened.

    B. I want revenge. It had not occurred to me that God could take care of my need for justice in a better way than I could.

    C. I have been trying to change the other person first.

    D. I never thought of that person as having low self-esteem, too. (It may not show on the surface.) I did not understand that was why that person is not able to affirm my self-esteem.

    E. It seems easier to blame myself and be depressed than to admit that person is at fault. I feel guilty, selfish, disrespectful of authority, afraid of hurting someone or of being hurt, or uncomfortable blaming someone else, even when logically I know the other person is in the wrong. I need to give myself permission to see that someone else can be to blame.

F.   I never considered the possibility that I could have misinterpreted that person.

G.   I tried to forgive instantly by praying. When my attitude of forgiveness did not last, I did not know what else to do. I felt discouraged. I need to let forgiveness be a goal toward which I can keep making progress.

H.   When people in authority make mistakes, I fail to show them the same mercy I do other human beings.

I.   The person who wronged me will not admit it and places all the blame on me. Then I feel even angrier and have more for which I have to forgive that person. I need to forgive this person for being unwilling to admit personal blame and for defensively attacking me more.

J.   It seems clear that my critical person is not going to change and will continue to hurt me. I have thought that if I forgave, I was supposed to forget, too, and act as though the person is not that way. If I closed my eyes to the reality of how that person treats me and did not protect myself, I would get hurt repeatedly. I did not know I could forgive and still take care of myself responsibly.

K.   I saw only what my critical person did to me. I did not realize I was being a critical person in return by not forgiving.

L.   Other. (Please describe.)

Is there someone you would like to ask to help you overcome your hurdle to forgiveness?

5. Have you ever forgiven someone who put you down? If so, what insights helped you forgive? Did forgiveness help you to stop believing his critical message was true?

# 3
# HOW DO I RECOGNIZE
# AND REWRITE TAPES?

Johnny Carson's nationally televised program "The Tonight Show" celebrates its anniversary each year by rerunning selected clips from its previous shows. Highlights are chosen from the program's best and worst moments. The results are hilarious.

The preparation for these rerun medleys obviously requires that archives be kept of the videotapes from the more than twenty-year history of this popular show. Someone must take responsibility for rating the tapes for worthiness of replay. The producers cannot help some of the things the actors serendipitously did in the original shows, but they can choose which tapes the audience will reexperience, and they can try to upgrade new videotaped shows in the future.

## I Am Responsible
The archives for personal recorded experiences are our brains, the locus of our critical tapes. These memories do not self-destruct. In addition, no one can perform brain surgery that will cut out only that part of our gray matter that stores particular tapes. What we can do, however, is to learn how to stop replaying them and to replace them with self-affirming beliefs.

Originally, others gave us harmful messages; thus, they are held responsible. However, now that we are adults, if we continue to play these tapes to ourselves, *we* are responsible.

I once heard a radio psychologist[1] tell her listeners that she used to blame her parents for all her problems. Around

45

her thirtieth birthday, she finally decided it was her own fault for allowing her problems to continue. *Each of us has to accept final responsibility for his or her own self-image.*

In a way, accepting responsibility can give us our first ray of hope. If my continued low self-esteem is someone else's responsibility, such as my parents', then I can change only if I can somehow get them to change first and affirm me. However, my self-image no longer depends on the critical persons who originally taught it to me. The present status of my self-esteem is up to me.

Since I have control over whether I decide to change my self-image, there is hope. I can prayerfully commit myself to taking whatever steps I need to heal any current brokenness regarding how I think of myself. As one of my counselees put it, "What a relief! I don't have to fix my parents first in order to fix myself."

The three steps of accepting responsibility for the ongoing condition of our self-esteem, of understanding the source of our low self-esteem, and of emotionally detaching from bad tapes by forgiving our critical persons provide half the cure.

The other half is to go back to the studio, set aside the old tapes, and record new ones.

## How Do I Think?

The Scriptures clearly encourage us to evaluate our thoughts. We do not have the luxury of anchoring any kind of thought that happens to coast through our minds. What we meditate on is what we are or become.

Proverbs 23:7 indicates that what a person thinks in his or her heart is what that person really is. In Romans 12:2, the Apostle Paul admonishes us to renew our minds.

What does a renewed mind think about? Paul provides the ideal in Philippians 4:8: "Finally, brethren, whatever is true, whatever is honorable, whatever is right, whatever is pure, whatever is lovely, whatever is of good repute, if there is any excellence and if anything worthy of praise, let your mind dwell on these things."

Critical tapes do not pass the test. Paul gives us little choice: they have to go. Obviously, there is one exception. We have to think about our destructive thoughts sufficiently to evaluate them in order to free ourselves of them.

Locating tapes sounds easy enough, but what do you do when the storage shelves and the playback equipment are in your own mind? Four things can help:

1. You turn up the "speakers" and listen very carefully.

2. Consciously notice what you say to yourself when you degrade yourself.

3. Log the content. Try writing down the actual sentences you say to yourself, names you call yourself, and feelings you relive when experiencing low self-esteem. This exercise will help you become well-acquainted with the precise content of your tapes.

---

**Examples of Common Self-Critical Tapes:**

"My feelings are stupid."

"There's nothing interesting about me."

"I can't do anything right!"

"Ugly me."

"No one could love me!"

---

One woman noticed that she felt like a nobody whenever anyone criticized her. She discovered that at those moments, she was saying to herself, "What's wrong with me? After all I have given you, it doesn't seem good enough to make your love come back to me!"

Another example is a man who expresses self-hatred by exclaiming, "What kind of Christian do I think I am! How could God ever love me?"

4. An additional way to discover the content of our self-critical tapes is to ask, "What criticisms do I believe others are

thinking about me?" Sometimes our answers to this question are based on our own tapes and will help us get to know their content. For instance, are you ever conscious of thinking any of the following?

"What must people think of me now?"

"I just know everyone is sure my head is full of air instead of brains!"

"If I'd stop putting on a show and really be myself, people would think I'm boring."

Such thoughts may be clues to our own self-talk or tapes.

A young bride who believed she was unattractive was sure her husband would one day leave her for some beautiful woman. All his sincere reassurances were to no avail. Finally, she realized the one who believed she was not an adequate enough woman to keep her man was not her husband, but herself.

The ways we imagine others are looking down on us may actually be the ways we are devaluing ourselves. Any "put-down" we use to attack ourselves or make ourselves feel valueless or unlovable is a critical tape.

Become well acquainted with any statement of self-rejection or self-hatred, any unmerciful or unforgiving attitude you inflict upon yourself.

*Halt the Reply.* Once we recognize our critical tapes, we can begin to learn how to stop them. Stopping the replay is a new habit that comes with practice.

Some people feel that it takes tremendous effort at first. One woman said, "I feel as though I have to stop my critical tapes a hundred times a day! It's exhausting. I'll never have energy to do anything else again if I keep this up." But like any skill it gets easier with practice. Eventually it becomes second nature.

At first, you may recognize the critical tape only after you have been replaying it for several minutes, hours, or even days or weeks. No matter how long it has been, stop playing it as soon as you recognize it. Gradually, you will get better at recognizing it earlier and earlier. *The goal is to learn to recognize and stop the replay as soon as the first self-rejecting thought begins.*

*Backsliding.* Despite our best efforts, we will backslide from time to time.

A man whose critical tape required him to "be perfect" to feel likable noticed that each time he replayed his perfectionism tape, he rejected himself for not being perfect at stopping the replay. He gave himself low self-esteem for giving himself low self-esteem! By discouraging himself for backsliding, he pulled the rug out from under himself.

Still, he wanted to understand his backsliding. He wondered, *What causes tapes to replay? To stop replaying? When I am on the road in this process of developing my self-worth, and then I regress — go backwards — have I lost everything I had before? Do I have to start all over again to pull myself up?*

Through careful observation, he discovered he was more prone to replay critical tapes when special circumstances made him more vulnerable. For example, one time he burned the "midnight oil" to complete an emergency work report and so did not get enough sleep. Next, he missed lunch in order to settle a dispute, and he was hungry. His boss was on his case. Everything went wrong at once.

Being fatigued and experiencing others assaulting his worth, he was more vulnerable to self-criticism. At times like these, he would think, *I always suspected I couldn't handle this job. Now I've proved it.* Then like clockwork, the old tapes would roll — "I am less because I am not perfect. . . . "

All was not lost. As he began to recognize the pattern, he would catch himself in it earlier and earlier each time it recurred. His periods of misery became shorter. Eventually, he gave himself permission to use each instance of backsliding as one to learn from, no matter how many times it happened.

Backsliding was only a reminder for him to pick up where he left off. It was not a matter of having to start all over again. By accepting his imperfection during the process of improving, he could still regard himself as lovable. In this way he could make progress.

Replaying the old tapes will happen occasionally as long as we live. How hard or how easy it is to get back on the track depends on several factors: (1) how strong the tapes were in the first place, (2) how accurately we understand their origin, (3) how much we were under attack when we backslid, (4) how much support or encouragement we have from others, and (5) most important of all, how motivated we are to change how we feel about ourselves.

Realistic expectations about backsliding will keep us from feeling devastated when it occurs. We can still live with lots of hope.

## Record Affirming Tapes

After shelving an old critical tape, replace it with a positive one. Ultimately, the secure basis for self-affirming tapes is what God says about us, but we can also profit from the positive messages that we get from one another. We simply may not be allowing ourselves to notice, or to benefit from positive feedback. If we expect rejection, it is likely that we will not let ourselves get close to others from the start and thus fail to get the affirmation we so much need.

(There is a potential danger of looking upon others as movie screens onto which we project the image of the critical persons of our past. In this way, we may see others as being like our critical persons even when they are not.)

*Give People a Chance.*  One day a woman in my office confided that all her life she had felt that she was an imposition on her parents, who had given birth to her late in their lives. In fact, whenever she needed anything, she assumed others resented it. That day as she and I talked, she asked me to write a very brief letter for her. Doing so was no trouble at all for me, yet she confessed her fear that I, too, was resenting her need. Because she overgeneralized from her critical persons to me, she blocked herself from recognizing help willingly given.

50

Love had been shown to her in many little ways by her family, friends, and myself, but she had to open herself to seeing it so that she could indelibly record our loving messages in her heart and mind. She could thereby experience and know that she was a loved and lovable person. Because her expectation was that everyone was like the critical persons in her life, she was not noticing when others showed their own positive feelings about her.

In a similar way, all of us need to give people a chance – to let them show by their own behavior whether they are accepting or not. In other words, we should not automatically assume people are personally against us. While there are going to be a few people who will be like the central critical persons of our past, most will not be. We should not make people start out with two strikes against them.

Think about this:

> *Most people are more anxious about whether we are going to accept them than about whether they are going to accept us.*

We are not the only ones concerned about acceptance. Those who are the most critical probably need the most affirmation as well.

When we do run across someone who degrades us again, we can deal with that person as we did with the critical persons of our past (as we discussed in the previous chapter). In other words, we need to forgive him or her, remembering the truth about our worth that replaces that person's critical message. When others do not love us unconditionally, we can still love them unconditionally. That's because God loves us, and that love settles our worth.

We retain our worth even when we run across an unloving person who does not happen to know our value at the moment. We can weather these inevitable incidents of life, provided we remember how to respond to them.

*Stop Discounting Positive Feedback.* We must learn to accept positive feedback. People say positive things to us, but if their affirming messages do not fit our preconceptions, we tend to reject them.

While waiting to speak on self-esteem at an evening church service, I sat up front next to the pastor while the congregation sang hymns. When he later introduced me, he referred to my having a "beautiful alto voice."

To understand my reaction to his compliment, it is important that you know that I had been kicked out of singing lessons by my voice teacher when I was a teenager. My teacher had broken the news to me as nicely as he could: I had "tried very hard, but. . . ." The bottom line was that I was not endowed with the best-quality vocal equipment.

Thus, when the pastor complimented me, do you think it was easy for me to accept it? Of course not. I thought, *He's just being nice. What else could he say? He needed something to say for the introduction.*

I proceeded to get up and, ironically, began speaking on how low self-esteem is healed. Then I came to my point about how we should stop discounting positive feedback. I shared my experience about the pastor's compliment and explained that I was having difficulty letting it sink in. It did not fit the way I was programmed to think about that part of myself. I, like others, had the problem of discounting positive feedback.

What did I say was the solution to my problem? *Consider the sincerity of the person who gave the compliment.* "For example," I said, turning with a "straight face" toward the pastor, who was beloved by his congregation and well-known for affectionately teasing others, "I could ask myself, 'Is the pastor *normally* a liar or a flatterer?' " (The congregation howled with laughter.) "Probably not. So I can at least believe that *he* believes the compliment. That's a place to start. Then maybe with time, I myself will begin to believe his affirming message." The point had been made.

*Recall Loving Tapes.* Not all the childhood messages about our worth were necessarily critical ones. The mere fact that we are alive means that someone cared about us at least enough to feed, bathe, clothe, protect, and instruct us when we were helplessly dependent children. Sandwiched between the negative messages were very likely some positive, loving tapes.

Sometimes it takes careful thought to remember them, however. This was true for Bonnie, who had the distinct impression that she had been an unwanted child. Her parents had divorced, and her mother had remarried a man who was an unkind and violent stepfather. After the birth of a half-brother, Bonnie was repeatedly reminded that she was less valuable. It was made clear to her that the only reason the family kept her was because "no one else would want you." Her half-brother was favored, while she was made to feel unimportant.

"The only thing I learned," she said, "was to survive in a world where there was no love, no touching, no closeness." She recalls no positive messages whatever about her worth from her family.

Nevertheless, Bonnie did receive some affirming messages. In her neighborhood was a Christian family that loved her. She would eat meals at their house and go to church with them. Their youngest daughter became her best friend. The mother, Mary, also became close to Bonnie and was aware of her situation.

Bonnie recalls, "She was there for me. If I had troubles at home, I'd go visit and just be with her. I felt better when I talked with her, like I really wasn't a bad person and was just going through some growing pains. With them, I felt loved and lovable. They showed me affection. I was made to feel a part of someone's family. I belonged.

"When I think of Mary and her family now, I have a very pleasant feeling. At times, I've asked myself, 'What would Mary say or do?' I have replayed her advice as I was growing up."

Bonnie recognized that she had some loving tapes about her value. Capitalizing on these, she based her self-image on loving tapes, instead of on the critical messages she got from home.

Some people find they have to look very carefully indeed to find any loving messages at all. Perhaps there was a relative, a schoolteacher, or a Sunday school or catechism teacher who cared. One man could think only of a Christian television personality who showed love. The preacher was a total stranger, but one who inspired him to begin speaking of himself as he believed that pastor would if given the opportunity.

## Summing It Up

We overcome low self-esteem by mentally tracing down our critical persons, understanding them, and forgiving them. We thereby free ourselves of the resentment that has enslaved us to their critical messages.

Next, we must stop listening to our self-critical tapes. Doing so requires that we accept responsibility for our self-esteem, identify our self-critical tapes, halt the replay, and cope positively with backsliding.

But we also need to identify affirming tapes and to use them for our benefit. By recalling constructive childhood memories and opening our ears to positive feedback in the present, we discover our affirming tapes.

In short, the steps to healing low self-esteem are forgive and retape.

Most importantly, in creating affirming tapes, we can believe God and build new self-image tapes based on what God says about us and on his love for us. Our heavenly Father is our only perfect parent and the only totally reliable source of information about our worth. God's love is unconditional and therefore is the only completely secure basis for our self-esteem.

We have already seen what God says about forgiving those who have hurt us. In subsequent chapters we will see how God meets our needs for the basic triad of self-esteem: feelings of belongingness, worthiness, and competence. What

God says forms the basis for completely trustworthy, affirming messages in these three areas. The next chapter discusses what God says about our belongingness.

## Target Questions

1. If you have a low self-image in some way, whom have you been blaming? Who should accept responsibility for maintaining the problem now?

2. What is the content of your critical tapes? That is, what sentences do you say to put yourself down? For example, how would you describe yourself, and do you accept yourself as you are? How do you think other people see you? What feelings do you experience when you degrade yourself?

3. Have you ever started to be unmerciful to yourself and stopped it? Describe how you did it.

4. Did you ever start to change and then backslide? What circumstances contributed to your going backward? How discouraged were you? Did you think you had lost everything you ever learned? Were you punishing yourself or being merciful to yourself? Did you give up or resume applying what helped before?

5. To what extent have you been assuming people you do not even know will be critical persons? What are the specific ways in which you expect people will be negative toward you? What do you think would happen if you gave people a chance to be who they really are, instead of living by your untested assumptions about them?

6. Do you discount some kinds of positive feedback? What kinds of compliments do you tend to reject? Do those types of compliments clash with your self-image? Is the person giving these compliments a liar, or is this person sincere? Can

you at least accept that the other person believes the compliment that he or she is giving?

7. Remember the most loving messages you've ever received. Who loved you and helped you feel you belonged? Who helped you feel like a good or lovable person even when you did something wrong? Who helped you believe you could do some things well?

8. When you replay your critical tapes, what loving messages do you want to use to replace them?

# 4
# HOW CAN I BELONG?

A young couple made a trip to Holland, the homeland of their ancestors. The wife was meeting her father's relatives for the first time. Her father had died in America when she was three, and she had no memories of him or his Dutch family.

One day while sightseeing, she and her husband spotted a grocery truck on a Dutch village street. (A grocery truck in Holland is like a "mom and pop" grocery store on wheels.) The truck stopped in front of a house, whereupon a housewife came out to buy her groceries. Delighted by this novel scene, the American couple went up very close to take a picture. Afterward, the husband wanted to explore the nearby alley. Although his wife protested, "It's somebody's backyard. I don't think we should go there," they went anyway.

Several days later, they visited the home of some relatives in another town. Many relatives had gathered to meet the couple, and the American wife told the story about seeing their first grocery truck. One of the aunts suddenly exclaimed, "I saw you there! The house was my house, the alley was my backyard, and I was the woman at the truck! When I looked into your face, I thought you looked familiar to me, though I had never met you!" The American woman resembled her paternal ancestors, even though she had never realized it. She bore the image of her father's family.

Sometime ago, a man named Alex Haley decided that he wanted to trace his roots, to find his ancestors and discover who he belonged to and to get a sense of who he was.[1] The result of his search was the book called *Roots*, which was turned into the well-known television mini-series tracing his lineage to the people to whom he belonged.

If we traced the roots of all of us, we would find that ultimately they go back to God who created us, and he created us in his own image, just as a father would. A father creates children who are like himself. That is what God has done with us. Our roots go back to him so that we rightfully should have a sense of belonging and identity with him.

Genesis 1:26 gives us this insight. This is one of the first things we have recorded that God wanted us to know.

> *Then God said, "Let Us make man in Our image, according to Our likeness; and let them rule over the fish of the sea and over the birds of the sky and over the cattle and over all the earth, and over every creeping thing that creeps on the earth." And God created man in His own image, in the image of God He created him; male and female He created them.*

Only a few chapters later, we read that much as God made humankind, male and female, in his likeness and image, similarly Adam fathered a son, Seth, in Adam's own likeness and image (Genesis 5:1-3). The parallel shows that God, as a father, created us to resemble, astonishingly enough, himself. In addition, since Adam, who was the image of God, created Seth in Adam's image, Seth would have been the image of God, too. This passage, therefore, seems to imply that the image of God is transmitted in the human species from parent to offspring.[2]

Theologians have debated what it means for man to have been made in the image of God, but virtually all agree that this image is what man shares with God, what distinguishes man from animals, and what causes man to be glorious and majestic. Most theologians further describe the image of God as including the personality of man characterized by self-consciousness, intellect, emotions, and a free will to make moral decisions.

The image of God is generally understood to describe the spiritual nature of man, but the body may be included in the image in that the Bible says man – not merely the soul of man – was created in God's image. The body is the suitable instrument for the self-expression of the soul, and the body is destined in the end to become a spiritual or heavenly body (1 Corinthians 15:29-49). Virtually all theologians agree that the created image of God included man's original sinless state and meant the sharing of God's holiness.[3] (The terms *image* and *likeness* seem to mean the same thing.)

At the time of the Protestant Reformation (in the sixteenth century), some theologians held the view that the image of God was lost in the Fall (when man sinned in Genesis 3). According to this theory, the image of God included only man's original state of holiness, not man's other spiritual characteristics that are like God's – things like intellectual powers, emotions, and free will. Therefore, when man sinned and lost his moral innocence, he ceased to be in the image of God.

But is that true? I do not think it is, and neither do most theologians nowadays. The image was marred, but the Scriptures talk about men since the Fall as being made in God's image.[4] In Genesis 9:6, God said to Noah after the Flood, "Whoever sheds man's blood, by man his blood shall be shed, for in the image of God He made man." This passage seems to be referring to human beings existing after the Fall as being in the image of God. It also indicates that murdering a human is wrong. In stark contrast, comparable commandments against killing other creatures do not exist in Scripture. Only the murder of a human being is singled out, because this amounts to killing God in representational form.

The Ku Klux Klan (KKK), a racist organization that exists predominately in southern states of America, has been known to burn people in effigy. An effigy is an image or likeness of a person. When the KKK wishes to terrorize someone, a large group of members may congregate in front of that person's home at night and erect a dummy or crude representational form of the individual they despise. They may then use lighted torches to set that image on fire in public protest against that person.

Similarly, when someone murders a human being, he or she is killing God in effigy. In fact, whatever we do to another human being we are doing to God in representational form, because even sinful human beings are still God's image.

The Apostle James sheds more light on this matter (in James 3:9) when he refers to the misuse of the tongue in abusive speech. "With it [the tongue] we bless our Lord and Father, and with it we curse men, who have been made in the likeness of God. . . ." Sometimes people think the reason it is wrong to curse people is only because we should not curse. However, James is adding a new facet: When we curse someone, we are cursing the image of God.[5]

When people attack our worth, they are, in effect, cursing the representational form of God. We remain in God's image, even though it is marred by our sin and even though critical persons may have failed to treat us as the infinitely valuable persons that we are. We do matter, whether others are able to recognize that or not. Our very nature and existence is rooted in God, and in that way, we belong to him.

### Lords and Ladies of Creation

As images of God, we have a relationship to the Creator that also points to our lordship over the earth and to our relationship to the creation.[6] Our dominion over the earth is another part of what makes us unique. Our destiny as Earth-rulers seems to set us apart from both the animals and the angels.

As far as we can discern from Scripture, the angels were not created to be lords of creation (though they sometimes appear to be represented as such) as humans were. By contrast, the angels are said to have been created as ministering spirits (Hebrews 1:7-8) sent to serve those who will inherit salvation.[7] However, human beings are the kings and queens of Earth.

When Prince Charles and Princess Diana's fairy-talelike marriage ceremony was televised before the world, it was hailed as "the wedding of the century." Many of us tried to imagine what it would be like to be royalty.

We do not have to settle for the imaginary. The Bible reveals that all members of the human race are royalty— Earth-rulers in the noble line of Adam and Eve. The human species is the sovereign family of Earth, and "blue blood" flows through our veins. Our coronation, decreed by God at our creation, is recorded in Genesis 1:27-28:

> *And God created man in His own image, in the image of God He created him; male and female He created them. And God blessed them; and God said to them, "Be fruitful and multiply, and fill the earth, and subdue it; and rule over the fish of the sea and over the birds of the sky, and over every living thing that moves on the earth."*

God formed us in his image so that we, like him, could rule. It used to be true more often than it is now that a father would train his children in his line of work so that they could run his business. In a sense, that is what God has done with us by putting us in charge of his creation. Sovereignty is our calling as human beings, and that gives us dignity, nobility, and majesty.

Every one of us is in the royal line of succession and has been called to rule our planet in some way. Below are a few of the more positive things we do to creation as we exercise our rulership over it. We:

| | | |
|---|---|---|
| Assemble it. | Categorize it. | Channel it. |
| Automate it. | Clean it. | Clothe it. |
| Beautify it. | Celebrate it. | Compute it. |

| | | |
|---|---|---|
| Construct it. | Hunt it. | Regulate it. |
| Cook it. | Imitate it. | Repair it. |
| Decorate it. | Loan it. | Seed it. |
| Distribute it. | Mine it. | Sell it. |
| Draw it. | Move it. | Shelter it. |
| Educate it. | Pave it. | Study it. |
| Energize it. | Populate it. | Tame it. |
| Entertain it. | Photograph it. | Traverse it. |
| Feed it. | Predict it. | Verbalize it. |
| File it. | Preserve it. | Weed it. |
| Govern it. | Record it. | Xerox it. |
| Heal it. | Reap it. | Zone it. |

Many of our activities in work, recreation, family living, and ministry are ways we rule creation every day.

Recently, I had the opportunity to explain the meaning of dominion to a friend of mine who is nine years old. Shortly before Halloween, she was showing me her costume, a pretty, light blue floor-length gown. She explained, "That's mother's dress, and Grandmother is going to hem it." There was also a band of gold sequins. "This is my crown. Mother and I are going to put blue and white flowers on it. And this is my scepter. We found it at a ballet equipment shop. I'm going to be a princess!"

I asked, "Did you know you really are a princess?" She smiled with embarrassment and said, "I read in a book that all sweet girls are princesses, and Mom and Dad say I'm sweet." I agreed. "And you are a princess in another way, too. The Bible says God made us humans to be the rulers of Earth. All of us are princesses and princes. Do you know what it means to be a princess of Earth?" She shook her head. I explained, "Did you ever plant a seed?"

She nodded and answered, "I planted a little tomato bush and it grew to be enormous!"

"That," I said, "is one way you ruled Earth. You ruled over that little plot of ground by deciding what would grow there. Another way you rule as a princess is by going to school. You study science, math, history, art, and language. You are learning how things operate on Earth so that when you grow up, you will know how to work and try to make the earth a better place. You are a real princess." She saw how the meaning of dominion in Genesis 1 applied to her.

I am awed by the commentary in Psalm 8:3-8, which celebrates this creation passage in Genesis. The psalmist begins by posing some negative questions that he later answers:

> *When I consider Thy heavens, the work of Thy fingers, the moon and the stars, which Thou hast ordained; what is man, that Thou dost take thought of him? and the son of man, that Thou dost care for him?*

These questions may remind us of our own sense of wonder as we have on occasion been away from the city lights and observed the endless galaxies in the night sky. We feel so insignificant, like mere ants or specks in the universe. We, like the psalmist, may ask, "How could God even notice us? And what is our place in the universe?"

The psalmist answers these questions, saying, "Yet Thou hast made him a little lower than God, and dost crown him with glory and majesty!" You and I are the crowning glory of the universe, the peak of creation, called to rule it with majesty.

Although we may not readily see our noble identity, we may struggle, even when we do, to make our "head knowledge" become "heart knowledge." It is one thing to have a textbook knowledge of who we are; it is another to trust it emotionally. Letting the truth penetrate us will give us affirming tapes and lift our self-esteem. We are in the image of God, kings and queens of the earth!

Some Christians may hesitate to spread the news that we are in the image of God. I have seldom heard a sermon on the nobility of man. Perhaps we are so concerned for people to know that they are sinners and that they are in need of the

Savior that we are afraid to talk about their nobility. Yet, God's regal image is what we are. It is our very essence.

Far from rejecting us as some human parents may do, we have seen that God the Father chose to bring us into our existence as his image and as rulers of the earth. We belong in his creation. We come from him, we are like him, and we share his nobility. He has elevated us to the most special position as kings and queens of creation.

"But," you might be protesting, "if every human has value because he or she is a human, then that means even criminals have value. Surely you don't mean that, do you?"

That is exactly what I mean. Even Adolf Hitler and Jack the Ripper bore the image of God. They, too, were lords of creation. Unfortunately, they applied their magnificent capacities to accomplish great evil.

The royal image of God is capable of decisions and acts of awesome significance — whether for good or ill. The potential of the human being to perform terrible evil also shows what a wondrous being the human is. If even the most vile of humans is God's marvelous, regal image, then you and I can rest assured that no matter what we may do, we are, too.

## Spiritual Birth

The truth of what we are stands, despite the fact that sin has marred our likeness to God and our ability to rule the earth as we ought. Adam and Eve joined Satan's rebellion against the Creator (Genesis 3:1-7). What were the results? Fear of God and hiding from his presence (Genesis 3:8-11). They experienced, for the first time, feelings of insecurity, separation, and lack of belongingness. Not only that, but ruling the earth became more difficult, because the earth, like its human lords and ladies, was cursed with imperfections. Work in the form of making a living or child-rearing became a mixture of joy and suffering (Genesis 3:16-19).

Who among us, like our ancestors Adam and Eve, has not sinned? Every member of our species has chosen to rebel against our loving Father Creator, rather than to share his moral perfection (Romans 3:10-12, 23). While God is still our Father in the sense that he created us and we are his image – a fact which nothing can take from us – we have all alienated or separated ourselves from his friendship and leadership.

In order to restore the leadership to God that each person has severed by rebellion and disobediencce, it is necessary to undergo a spiritual birth (John 1:13; 3:1-8) by receiving God's forgiveness and joining his spiritual family or spiritual kingdom. As the Apostle John says, "But as many as received Him [Jesus], to them He gave the right to become children of God, even to those who believe in His name" (John 1:12). After we receive forgiveness through Jesus, God fathers us not only as the Creator and giver of natural life, but also as the giver of spiritual and eternal life. We are then connected to him more completely.

In John 17:9, when Jesus was saying his last good-byes to his closest friends before his death, he prayed to his Father about all who would follow him, declaring, "They are Thine!" We belong to God.

Romans 8:15-16 says that God's Spirit cries out within us, "Daddy, Father," because we know we are his children. We all naturally belong to God our Father as his creatures, but also, if we wish, as his children born into his spiritual family. For those of us who have made this choice, "Our Father who art in Heaven" (Matthew 6:9) is the perfect parent. God attends to his children rather than neglecting them, and he never abandons or ridicules his spiritual offspring. We can receive affirming, healing messages from him that can correct the impact of harmful messages we may have received as children.

## God's Loving Attention
We know we belong because our Father God tenderly pays attention to us. This is well documented in Scripture. The psalmist says, for example,

*O Lord, Thou has searched me and known me. Thou dost know when I sit down and when I rise up; Thou dost understand my thoughts from afar, Thou dost scrutinize my path and my lying down, and art intimately acquainted with all my ways. Even before there is a word on my tongue, behold, O Lord, thou dost know it all. Thou has enclosed me behind and before, and laid Thy hand upon me. Such knowledge is too wonderful for me; it is too high, I cannot attain to it. . . .*

*For Thou didst form my inward parts; Thou didst weave me in my mother's womb. I will give thanks to Thee, for I am fearfully and wonderfully made; wonderful are Thy works, and my soul knows it very well. . . . When I awake, I am still with Thee.* (Psalm 139:1-6, 13-14, 18)

Here the psalmist celebrates God's attentiveness. God is intimately acquainted with all our ways. He was lovingly thinking of us when we brushed our teeth this morning and will still be attending to us when we pull back the bedcovers tonight. He was thinking of us when we were conceived and when we were born, and he will continue to do so when we grow old and when we die.

Jesus said in Matthew 10:30, when he was talking about how much attention our Father gives us, "But the very hairs of your head are all numbered." He knows how many hairs are on my head. I myself don't even care! But he does. He even knows how many we lose.

One time when I spoke on this verse, a woman humorously called out from the back row, "Does he know how many are falling out?" He knows. That is how much loving attention he is giving us.

Psalm 56:8 tells us, "Thou hast taken account of my wanderings; put my tears in Thy bottle; are they not in Thy book?" He knows when we cry, and yes, he cares.

Father God does not neglect his children, those who have placed themselves into his loving hands.

*No Abandonment.* Consider what David records about his family in Psalm 27:10: "For my father and mother have forsaken me, but the Lord will take me up."

David indicates that he felt abandoned by his parents, and with good reason. When the prophet Samuel came to anoint one of Jesse's sons as king, Jesse paraded all of David's brothers before the prophet and left David out tending the sheep, even though Samuel had explicitly invited all of Jesse's sons to come. Samuel had to ask whether Jesse had yet another son somewhere. Evidently, Jesse believed that David would never amount to anything (1 Samuel 16).

Later, when David was sent on an errand to take food to his brothers in the army that was unsuccessfully opposing Goliath and the Philistines, his older brothers belittled him for presuming that God could use him to help Israel prevail against her enemies (1 Samuel 17:26-29). Nothing is known concerning David's mother, but some commentators have gathered that he may have been born out of wedlock.[8]

Though rejected by his family, David as a shepherd boy experienced security, love, and belongingness as he experienced God as his own Shepherd and Father (Psalm 23).

God intended our human parents to serve as pictures of what he is like as our divine parent. Unfortunately, this analogy is not always helpful, as the Scriptures recognize. Isaiah says, for instance, "Can a woman forget her nursing child, and have no compassion on the son of her womb? Even these may forget, but I will not forget you" (Isaiah 49:15). God never abandons any child born into his family. As clear evidence, the original language in Hebrews 13:5 is most emphatic and might best be translated: "I will never, never desert you. No, I will not ever, ever leave you." Unlike some human parents, our heavenly Father will never turn his back on us.

*No Ridicule.* God will not ridicule us either, even though we may suppose he will. A man once told me that as a boy he had a recurring, frightening dream of a picture of Christ that hung in his bedroom. In this dream, the eyes in the picture would look at him and the face of Christ would start laughing, as if to say, "You're kidding! You in the same room with my picture? You in my church? Ha!" The persisting dream became so troubling that his mother finally had to remove the picture. He had refused to enter his room if the lights were on.

This dream was, in part, the result of his education. He had attended a parochial school that taught him to fear God. The implied message was "You'd better be perfect or you'll give God a flaw to laugh at." It did not help that his older brother unrelentingly looked for reasons to laugh at him, too. The idea of God ridiculing him, though, was, in his words, "the ultimate rejection." He explained, "Here's this Being you worship, but if you breathe wrong, you're dead, and there is nothing you can do about it. You are small, helpless, and terrified." As a boy, he believed God's watchful attention was not loving but critical and rejecting.

When he became a teenager, he experimented with youth groups of other churches. His purpose was "to find out if this problem was just in my church or in religion in general. To make a long story short, at one of these churches, I found a merciful God. I came to know he does not ridicule me, and now I love and serve him."

That God does not ridicule us is forcefully asserted by the Apostle James, who was the half-brother of Jesus. James experienced firsthand, as the brother of Christ (Matthew 13:55; Galatians 1:19), that God will not ridicule us. James says in his epistle, "If any of you lacks wisdom, let him ask of God, who gives to all men generously and without reproach, and it will be given to him" (James 1:5). The King James Version of this verse says God "upbraideth not." Both expressions, "without reproach" and "upbraideth not," mean God will not ridicule us.

No matter how sensitive or private we usually are about

68

our feelings, it is safe to open ourselves freely to God. If we imagine that he is sneering at us, this impression is not the conviction of the Holy Spirit. More than likely, we are actually listening to our own critical tapes with the assumption that these thoughts are from God.

Perhaps we had the misfortune of being taught that God is a "critical person" toward his own children. The fact is that God is not a rejecting Judge. Instead, he is a loving father to all who join his spiritual family. He calls everyone to come and join him, to choose to belong with him and to receive his love.

*No Favoritism.* Two adult sisters were discussing their views on whether God the Father "plays favorites" with his children. One speculated, "I think God secretly loves some people more. In fact, I hope he does. I always felt I was Mom's favorite. It's embarrassing to admit, but I guess I think that if some people were more special to God, I would be one of them."

"How can you say that!" her sister protested. "I don't want God to have favorites. I know I wasn't Mom's or Dad's favorite. So I'm scared that if God favors some people, I would be left out."

A woman from another family mysteriously experienced guilt whenever she was complimented. Careful reflection resulted in her discovering the insight that she felt guilty because she was her parents' favorite and because her father even seemed to prefer her to her mother. She sensed other family members suffered for her being favored. She felt somehow responsible. To her, favoritism was not a blessing, but a curse.

Does God favor some people and discriminate against others?

The Apostle Peter used to think so. God had to use visions and speak to him directly to show him otherwise. At last, Peter got the point. He concluded, "I most certainly understand *now* that God is not one to show partiality, but in every nation the man who fears Him and does what is right, is welcome to Him" (Acts 10:34-35).

Our heavenly Father is impartial and will not show preference to anyone who comes to him. We are equally "welcome to him."

## Summing It Up

In *The Sensation of Being Somebody*, Maurice Wagner introduced the concept that the various ways in which psychologists are aware that we need self-esteem can be reduced to the triad of belongingness, worthiness, and competence. He further perceived that the Triune God fulfills these needs. We belong because God the Father fathers us, we have worth because Jesus provides forgiveness for us, and we have competence because the Holy Spirit enables us as we cooperate with him.[9] The next three chapters will discuss more about worthiness and competence.

In this chapter, we have seen that God the Father fulfills our need for belongingness by fathering us as Creator and spiritual Father. He bestowed immeasurable value on us when he made us in his image and ordained us to rule the earth. Unlike human parents, he is the perfect Father and never rejects, neglects, abandons, ridicules, or discriminates against his spiritual children. He wants us to realize who we are and that we belong to him forever.

## Target Questions

1. In front of a mirror, address yourself by name, and say, "You are the image of God and a lord [or lady] of God's creation." See and hear yourself speak this truth.

2. Enumerate ways that you are ruling creation right now. You may wish to refer to the list of forty-five activities suggested earlier in this chapter. Consider activities you engage in for work, recreation, family living, and ministry. If you are

reading this book for a study group, allow group members to share their results and further expand each other's ideas.

3. Beginning with getting out of bed, go through one entire day reminding yourself, as you face each person and task, that you are the image of God and that each task you do is caring for God's creation in some way. Describe this experience.

4. On another day, remind yourself as you encounter people that each one is the image of God. Describe your experiences from these encounters.

5. Do you believe that every human being is the image of God and a lord or lady of creation? Do you believe this is true of wicked and unloving people? Is it true of your critical persons? How does your answer affect the ways you think of others and treat them?

6. If you are reading this book with a study group, have each group member turn to another group member and tell him or her, "You are the image of God and you are ruling his creation for him." Make sure each person has the opportunity to be told this.

7. Have you ever received God's forgiveness for your own sins and joined his spiritual family? If not, is there any reason why you would not like to tell God you are taking this step right now? If you have done so, thank God that you and he belong to each other.

8. As you grew up, did you feel (a) you received insufficient loving attention (that is, you were rejected or neglected), (b) you were abandoned, (c) you were ridiculed, or (d) you were favored or not favored? If so, you may wish to review the relevant section in this chapter and try to find a verse or concept that helps you.

71

Notice how your heavenly Father is different from your earthly parents. Perhaps you would like to memorize the helpful verse or concept or write it where you can refer to it frequently until it becomes a part of you. If the problem troubles you very deeply, perhaps you will wish to discuss it with your pastor or a trusted Christian friend or a counselor.

9.  Close in prayer by thanking God for making you in his image and creating you to help rule his creation. Thank him for always bathing you in his loving attention and for never leaving you or ridiculing you. Thank him that you belong to him and he belongs to you forever.

# 5
# HOW CAN I BE WORTHY?

My husband and I recently vacationed in Hawaii. One evening at sunset, while dining outdoors on a restaurant balcony on Waikiki beach, we were overwhelmed by the beauty of the scenery. Trees were in blossom, and phosphorescent waves rolled gently into shore. A warm tropical breeze carried sweet Hawaiian love songs and played with the lighted torches.

What must native life have been like before Captain Cook brought Western culture here? We pictured young Hawaiians falling in love on this beautiful island and leading tranquil lives of relative leisure. Fish, pineapples, coconuts, and guavas must have been abundant. The need for shelter must have been minimal because of the warm, even climate. Their gentle, romantic music suggested they were a peace-loving people. It must have been paradise, we thought.

A few days later, we picked up a book on Hawaii's history. The truth destroyed our idyllic fantasy. Power-hungry, greedy kings had constantly warred for supremacy over the islands, subjugating their neighbors and oppressing women and the poor. Finally, King Kamehameha had united the islands under his own rule that choreographed the execution of enemy warriors by hurling them off the cliff of Nuuanu Pali. The truth was that Hawaiian history had been filled with as much bloodshed, intrigue, and oppression as the history of any other people.[1]

I felt a sense of tragic loss when I realized the natives had never achieved paradise. What was true of the Hawaiians is true of the whole human race. The Scriptures say God created perfect humans in the Garden of Eden under paradiselike conditions, in a setting abounding with beautiful, glorious potential. And what did we do with that potential? We snatched defeat from the jaws of victory! Rebelling, we brought to our planet every kind of wickedness and suffering.

Nevertheless, there are remnants of the good and the lovely. We came from a state of blessedness and will, as Christians, dwell in such a state eternally. It seems God allows us to taste enough paradise on earth to know that paradise exists somewhere, but also enough hell on earth to let us know this place is not paradise.

## The Problem of Sin

Something is very wrong in our world, and that something is sin. Every one of us has joined the rebellion against God by sinning.

We thus find ourselves in a dilemma. As we have seen, each of us is the image of God and belongs to him as our Creator and, if we wish, as our spiritual Father. We are valuable because we belong to God, but we are also sinful. We tend to doubt our value, because we know God does not like sin.

As important as our belongingness is for self-esteem, we also need to see ourselves as good or morally worthy in order to have positive self-images. And since we sin, the question arises. "Are we really good?" What does the Bible say about the relationship between sin and healthy self-esteem?

In Genesis 1:31, God looked at all that he had created, particularly man, and said that "it was very good." Five chapters later, in Genesis 6:6, God was so grieved that he had ever made man that he decided to destroy all but eight human souls by a flood.

What had happened between these two events to change God's attitude from approval to grief? The answer, of course, is the Fall of man in Genesis 3. Humankind became sinful, and the image of God was tainted and distorted. Only eight people even sought God's forgiveness (Genesis 7:1, 7; 8:20).

What does sin do to the moral worthiness of a human being? Are we worthy of God's approval and acceptance? The Scriptures say no. In Romans 3:10-12a, the Apostle Paul quotes the ancient wisdom revealed in Psalms 14 and 53:

> *There is none righteous, not even one;*
> *There is none who understands,*
> *There is none who seeks for God;*
> *All have turned aside, together they have become useless . . .*

Some translations say *worthless,* instead of *useless,* which in the original language means "become depraved, worthless,"[2] and "unserviceable"[3] (in the sense of being damaged). For example, an automobile with a blown-up engine is still an automobile, but it is mechanically damaged and therefore worthless. Similarly, every one of us is morally damaged and worthless, though we are still images of God. As far as our moral and spiritual performance is concerned, we do not have what it takes to impress God. In that sense, he says we are worthless.

God does not "grade on the curve." His evaluation is strictly "pass" or "fail," "A" or "F," "perfect" or "imperfect." While we might rate ourselves as "good" in comparison to most people, God compares us to his own perfect holiness. Who can measure up to that standard? That is why Jesus said only one person is "good," and that is God (Luke 18:18-19). If we are honest, the more we get to know about God's moral perfection, the better we will realize that Jesus was right.

The Apostle Paul says we are all sinners (Romans 3:23), and our sinful condition makes us "useless" or "worthless." If that were all that the Scriptures said about our worthiness, this book would end and we would resign ourselves to miserable self-loathing.

## Forgiveness

Fortunately, we know that this is not where it all ends, because we can become worthy apart from our own deeds. We receive forgiveness by what Jesus has done for us. In 2 Corinthians 5:21, Paul proclaims that God made Jesus, who was sinless, to be sin that we might become the righteousness of God in him. God put our sins on Jesus and put Jesus' moral perfection on us. Jesus took the punishment for our sin when he died on the cross, and we are given credit for being as righteous as Jesus. On this basis, Paul says, we are forgiven for our sins. God's forgiveness is a gift we can receive if we wish.

We are worthy of God's approval because Jesus provided a solution. We have value because we are in God's image, but as far as our moral goodness or worthiness of approval is concerned, it is taken care of because Jesus saved us out of our dilemma.

When I was a girl, a story told by Ethel Barrett[4] helped me understand the meaning of Jesus' death. It went like this:

Once upon a time, there was a good king who ruled his kingdom wisely. He also had a son. This king made a law that no one was to do a certain deed; and if anyone broke this law, the punishment was to have both eyes put out.

One day, the king's own son broke that law. Grieved to the core, the king paced before his throne in agony. What could he do! He loved his son and could not bear to harm him. Yet he was a just and fair ruler and had to champion goodness and avenge evil. How could he be both loving and just?

He found a solution. Calling his court before him, he pronounced, "The law says if anyone breaks this law, two eyes will be put out. And two eyes shall be put out—one of my son's and one of my own."

In a similar way, God himself, in the form of his son, died on the cross and took our punishment. However, he did not merely take half of our punishment for us. He took all of it! By this means, God's justice was satisfied and we can receive his forgiveness.

God thought we were worth salvaging, despite our moral unworthiness. Why? Perhaps because we are His image. Or maybe because God is so loving. Although the Scriptures do not seem to make that reason clear, there is no mistaking that he loved us and wanted to undo the damage of sin and win us back. He was willing to pay a dear price. Clearly, he sets a very high value on us.

How do we know the value of an object? It is determined by the price someone is willing to pay for it. Not far from my home is an outdoor market where local artists peddle their wares on weekends. An artist may place a price tag on a painting for a hundred dollars. But if it sells for seventy-five dollars, that is the worth of the painting. The purchase price establishes the value.

Similarly, the price God was willing to pay for us was the suffering and death of his dearly loved Son, Christ Jesus: "For God so loved the world, that He gave His only begotten Son, that whoever believes in Him should not perish, but have eternal life" (John 3:16). The price God paid is the value he placed on us.[5] His price established our value. And what a value that is!

Jesus' death makes us worthy because he satisfied the penalty of sin and thereby provided the means for our forgiveness. In addition, his death established the value that we, even before we accepted that forgiveness, had to God.

*God Is Not Angry with Me.* After we receive God's gift of forgiveness and worthiness, God does not become angry at us when we sin.

A new Christian found herself caught in the nightmare of loving her husband's best friend. This crisis came to a crescendo when her husband was given notice at work that he would have to move out of state or lose his job with the company. She wondered whether to stay behind with her secret lover or move with her husband.

Guilt plagued her and her thinking was confused. While she thought her affair was wrong in the sense that it might make God angry with her, she did not draw the logical conclusion that because it was wrong, God's guidance would be for her not to continue it.

How she agonized for God to show her what to do! She studied every little event as a possible sign from God. Yet because she had sinned, she believed God was angry and would punish her by not helping her. It was up to her to muddle through as best she could. "God doesn't hear a sinner's prayer," she believed.

After I indicated that I, too, had heard that viewpoint about a sinner's prayer, I asked her, "Who of us is ever in a sinless state?" There is probably never a moment we are altogether free of sin, including unconfessed sin. We are not even aware of all our sin; so we never can confess it all. If we could not gain a relationship with God by our own actions, how could we maintain it by our own performance either?

Thankfully, our relationship with God always depends on what *Jesus* has done. While people may shut us out or give us "the silent treatment" when we sin against them, God does not make his fellowship with us depend on our spiritual condition. If he did, none of us would ever have fellowship with him. Rather, like the father of the Prodigal Son, God mercifully longs for us to repent and turn back toward him even while we are yet sinning (Luke 15:20).

I explained to this woman that the purpose of God's law in her life was not to make her sinless so that God would love her and be willing to help her in time of need. Instead, God's law provided the very guidance she sought. The commandment "You shall not commit adultery" (Exodus 20:14) was God's answer all along.

Is God angry with a Christian when he or she sins? Sometimes we think he is, but 1 John 2:2 says, "He [Jesus] Himself is the propitiation for our sins." That word *propitiation* means he is the satisfaction for our sins. We know the Scriptures talk about God's righteous wrath toward sin, but God took out his wrath on Jesus when Jesus died on the cross. God found a way to take care of his own anger, and he did so.

When we sin now, God is not a resentful parent who corrects us in anger or refuses to listen or talk to us. Sometimes a human parent will do these things, but our heavenly parent does not. Romans 8:1 says, "There is therefore now no condemnation for those who are in Christ Jesus." Put another way, there is no "shame on you," no dirty look.[6] Sometimes we mistakenly think God reacts that way or that the Holy Spirit is convicting us. Far from being the Holy Spirit speaking, however, it actually may be our critical tapes playing.

Revelation 12:10 says that Satan, the accuser of the saints, points a condemning finger, but God does not. Instead, God corrects us lovingly. Hebrews 12 tells us that he teaches us in love. He does not get even with us in anger.

*Why Be Good?* We do not have to be good and obey God's laws in order to get him to love us. He loves us unconditionally. Romans 5:8 says, "But God demonstrates His own love toward us, in that while we were yet sinners, Christ died for us." He loves us no matter what.

Well, then, why be good? Why not sin it up? Are Christians free to indulge in all their favorite sins? Sometimes it may seem so.

As a family was driving to church, daughter Janie (then eight and a half) announced, "Mom, Dad, did you know that Susie is a Christian now?"

"Well, that is good news . . . ," the mother began.

"I talked with her and explained it," Janie said earnestly, "and then she prayed."

"Yup," said four-year-old Susie, "I thanked God for *all* my sins!"

Choking back her laughter, Janie sputtered, "No, Susie, you asked God to *forgive* your sins!"

Looking bored, Susie gave an unconcerned wave of her hand. "God knows," she said cheerfully.[7]

How many people sound as though they are literally thankful for their sins? Think of all the times you have heard sin advertised as fun (or have done this yourself).

A well-known song that was number one on the charts in pop music radio advocated "faster horses, younger women, older whiskey, and more money."[8] C. S. Lewis, in *The Abolition of Man*,[9] refers to a fictional character who sold his soul to the devil for "gold and guns and girls."

A "take-off" on a hymn as sung by some rebels expresses the attitude this way:

> *Saved by grace,*
> *O happy condition!*
> *Free to sin,*
> *For there is remission.*

In other words, "Wheee!"

Paul realized that there would be a temptation to react this way to forgiveness, as ungrateful and calloused as this response may be. He addressed the problem this way: "Shall we sin more, so God can show his grace even better?" He answers, "Heavens, no!" (This is a paraphrase of Romans 6:1-2.)

Is sin really all the fun that Hollywood says it is?

Proverbs 23:17 warns, "Do not let your heart envy sinners. . . . " And Proverbs 14:12 clarifies, "There is a way which seems right to a man, but its end is the way of death." Sin is not living it up. It is self-destructive and harmful to others. Not only that, it hinders the progress of God's kingdom.

When you think about it, is there fulfillment or joy in envy, hatred, belligerence, verbal or physical violence, deceit, disloyalty to your mate, exploiting someone, greed, or enslavement to one's bodily drives? About all sin has to offer is (1) excessive or inappropriate gratification of impluses ("the lust of the flesh"), (2) accumulation, by wrongful means or motives, of things that leave the inner person hollow ("the lust of the eyes") and (3) inflated self-estimation created by denying one's need for God or by comparing one's money, power, prestige, or fortune (or misfortune) to others, whom one tends to devalue in the process ("the pride of life" – 1 John 2:16).

Jesus defined sin as the opposite of love (Matthew 22:36-40). It is love, Paul explains, that is accompanied by joy and peace (Galatians 5:22). Jesus wanted us to experience as much love and joy as he had (John 15:11-12).

The reason we obey God is because obedience benefits us. The psalmist celebrates the goodness of God's guidelines in Psalm 19:7-11. He uses several synonyms to stand for God's law. He calls it the "law," "testimony," "precepts," "commandment," and "judgments" of the Lord, and he explains what obedience to God's laws does for us.

"The law of the Lord is perfect, restoring the soul." It heals us psychologically as we obey from the heart.

"The testimony of the Lord is sure, making wise the simple." It makes us wise.

"The precepts of the Lord are right, rejoicing the heart." It gives us joy.

> *The commandment of the Lord is pure, enlightening the eyes. The fear of the Lord is clean, enduring forever; the judgments of the Lord are true; they are righteous altogether. They are more desirable than gold, yes, than much fine gold; sweeter also than honey and the drippings of the honeycomb.*

The psalmist goes on to summarize what God's laws do for us: "Moreover, by them Thy servant is warned; in keeping them there is great reward." Warning and reward. By keeping God's commandments, we avoid a lot of misery and bring ourselves joy and wisdom.

Do we obey God so that he can love us more? No! He already loves us as much as he can – which is totally.

## I Don't Have to Like All of Me
God loves us unconditionally, but do we love ourselves the same way?

81

Feeling worthy does not mean liking everything about ourselves. Let's be honest. Since we are still sinners (though forgiven), not everything about us is likable.

A woman whose sexual unfaithfulness had destroyed her marriage believed, despite it all, that she was a good person. After her husband divorced her, she continued her wayward life-style. In a counseling session one day she announced, "I have bad news. I found out I have Herpes, and it does not seem fair. Why me? I didn't do anything!"

I choked back my almost irresistible temptation to confront her because I had tried that approach with her on previous occasions and it had made little impact. I held my silence. Then she courageously admitted, "I brought it on myself. And now I may have infected others, too! And all because of my own selfishness. This is hard for me to face."

She was beginning to recognize that there were parts of herself she liked and parts of herself she did not like. This new perception worried her because she had always felt her worthiness depended on being good. She had not realized she could be sinful and still have value, indeed, that that is the only way any of us does have worth. Consequently, she had been rather defensive about admitting any significant faults.

Have you ever been defensive? That's a needless question, isn't it? Defensiveness as a way to save face has been with the human race since its original ancestors. After Adam and Eve sinned in the Garden of Eden, we are told in Genesis 3, they felt naked and exposed for the first time. The experience was so uncomfortable that they sewed together fig leaves and covered themselves. Then they hid. Even when God found them and confronted them, they still did not honestly face their own sin. Adam blamed Eve, who then blamed the serpent. Things have not changed much, have they?

God's merciful forgiveness and unchangeable love free us to look at our sin squarely and say, "Yes, that's part of me, too." If God, knowing all my sin, loves me, then I also can affirm my worth, sinner that I am.

There seems to be a universal temptation to think that either (1) all my actions are righteous (the defensive approach) and therefore I am deserving of love and approval, or (2) my actions are sinful and therefore I am worthless (the approach that leaves out Jesus). However, there is alternative: (3) my actions are sinful, yet because of Jesus' gift, God declares me worthy and so I am.

Jesus has saved us from having our worthiness measured by our own moral record. When we come to him to receive the gift of forgiveness and enter into his family, we have Jesus' moral perfection credited to our account. We no longer need to hide our sin from ourselves or him. We can be genuine, sincere, honest, real, and have our worth, too.

## What about "Self"?

*Old Self versus New Self.* Some fairly common misconceptions can create a problem for a Christian's sense of worthiness. They have to do with the idea of "dying to self."

Have you ever heard that phrase? Sometimes it is expressed this way: "If you take the word *flesh*, remove the *h*, and spell this word backwards, it spells *self*." The point of the saying is to equate the "flesh," a biblical term for the old sin nature or the desire in fallen man to sin, with the whole person. Therefore, one should die to sin by dying to self.

With what kind of self-image does this viewpoint leave a person? A bad one.

If we are believers in Jesus Christ, I think it is unscriptural to equate the whole self with the old self because the Bible says we have been given a new self. There is more to my self than the old sin nature. In fact, my real self is my new self that loves to do right and will live forever. I do not want to die to my new self, just to my *old* self, or my sinful desires. This clarification is essential.

In Romans 7, the Apostle Paul admits to an inner battle— he does wrong but yearns to do right. He begins in verse 18, "For I know that nothing good dwells in me. . . ." Some people put the period there, but not Paul. He says, "I know that nothing good dwells in me, that is, in my flesh." No good thing dwells in Paul's *old* self, but he does not think the old sinful nature is his real self. He clarifies, "But if I am doing the very thing I do not wish, I am no longer the one doing it, but sin which dwells in me" (v. 20). In fact, to show how good his new and real self is, he adds in verse 22, "I joyfully concur with the law of God in the inner man."

In the Apostle Paul and in all Christians, the new nature that loves to live God's way is the true moral nature that will live eternally. The love of sin is passing away and will finally end when the Christian goes to be with the Lord, receives his new body, and is "glorified" or made perfect like Christ (Romans 8:17-25, 29-30). When we receive forgiveness here on earth, we are credited with Jesus' perfection, though we will still sin. When we see Jesus in eternity, however, we will actually become morally perfect like him (1 John 3:2).

Understood correctly, dying to the old self means dying to selfishness. The overarching purpose of all we do now is to advance God's kingdom, in which we share.

Many Christians have been confused by the idea of dying to self. This concept greatly troubled me as a youngster growing up in the church. I wondered what it meant and whether it was a desirable goal. Many aspects of my life seemed to have little or no moral significance, such as my choice of a favorite color or the fact that I played the piano. I questioned, "Why should these facets of my self die? How would I go about dying to self anyway?"

I assumed I would have to cease to exist, yet I believed everyone exists eternally. The concept made no sense to me and puzzled me deeply. Now, of course, I realize that my self is the image of God, though not his perfect likeness presently because there is still sin in me. Obviously, I cannot die to being the image of God. I can only commit myself to the life-long process of learning to cleanse myself from sin.

Another confusing saying for self-worth is "When I sin, I get the credit. When I do what is right, Christ gets the credit."

Where does that leave a person's self-image? Not doing too well.

Again the solution to this misunderstanding is that we have a new self, as Paul explains in Ephesians 4:22-24. When I sin, my old self gets the credit, and when I do what is right, Christ and the new me get the credit. Now the new me ultimately comes from him, and he should get the glory for that. However, I am still the one who is doing what is right because he has given me a new self.

I am worthy because Jesus has forgiven me for my old sinful nature and has given me a new moral nature—a longing to be like him.

*The Renewed (Not Replaced) Self.* We have seen that a common misconception among Christians is that we become good by putting the self to death. Another version of this misconception is that we become holy by replacing our own personalities with the personality of Christ. Both versions imply that the whole personality, not just our sin, is unworthy of God's approval.

A man who seriously tried to let Christ replace his own inner self found his marriage in dire straits. His wife felt starved for meaningful companionship and wondered if there even was a real person residing inside his body. All she heard was "God's view" of this and "God's view" of that. What she desperately wanted to know was her husband's own thoughts and feelings. "Does he have any?" she pleaded.

It took several weeks of counseling for him to grasp what she was talking about. When he did, he was able to piece together what had led him to give up his own self. As he expressed it, he believed that if he acknowledged personal views and wishes that he thought differed from God's, then he would be showing lack of faith and giving the devil an opportunity to make his negative thoughts come true in some way. His way of trying to be like Christ was to drown his own imperfect personality and express only godly truth.

He could actually remember why he had decided to live

this way. His parents had been exceptionally critical whenever he spoke his mind. In self-defense, he had decided it would be much safer never to reveal his true feelings or develop his own unique personality. He would be what others would approve of. His critical tape said, "Don't be you. Don't think. Don't feel."

After learning he could be his real self again, he was both frightened and relieved. When he expressed his actual thoughts and feelings, he became considerably more interesting. The self he had been expressing may have been a reflection of God's true self to some extent, but it was a false self for him. His spiritual growth had been stunted because he had avoided experiencing the growing pains of helping his real self become more and more like Christ.

Wouldn't it be strange for God to give us the ability to reason, feel, and choose by making us in his own image and then tell us not to use these marvelous capacities? Unfortunately, this seems to be what some Christians believe God has done. They seem to think that, much as a hermit crab looks for a vacated shell in which to take up residence, so God looks for a human who is emptied of his or her own personality so that God's personality can fill that hollow human shell.

If we equate the inner self with the sin nature, we will try to become like Christ by eliminating our own reasoning, feelings, and wishes. We may view Christ as trying to replace ourselves.

If on the other hand, we define self as the image of God with the ability to utilize and to misuse our capacities sinfully, we will attempt to become like Christ by exercising our own reasoning, feelings, and wishes in a holy way. We will see Christ as making our self complete and good.

It is this last view that Paul teaches in Romans 12:1-2:

> I urge you therefore, brethren, by the mercies of God, to present your bodies a living and holy sacrifice, acceptable to God, which is your spiritual service of worship.

> *And do not be conformed to this world, but be transformed by the renewing of your mind, that you may prove what the will of God is, that which is good and acceptable and perfect.* (Emphasis added.)

When Paul pleads with us to sacrifice ourselves and not to conform to the world, he does not mean we should put to death our own personalities so that God's personality may take over. Rather, we are to present ourselves as a "living" sacrifice.

Our minds are to be changed, not exchanged or extinguished, in order that we may "prove" the will of God. The word *prove* in the original language means "discover," "try to learn," "examine," "be convinced of," "prove by testing," and "approve."[10] By such active means, God wants the Christian's own understanding and way of thinking to be transformed, not replaced.

Of course, this kind of maturity is not instantly achieved. It takes a lifetime of learning and examining before we wholeheartedly agree with God's ways. Meanwhile, we will not always see "eye to eye" with God, and thus we must obey him by faith until we can obey him with understanding. Obviously, when the Scriptures say, "Do not lean on your own understanding" (Proverbs 3:5), they do not negate the value of godly understanding, but only of erroneous understanding that diverges from God's.

Even after God finishes transforming us into the likeness of Christ, each of us will *still* have a unique self that is distinct from God himself and every other self. When Jesus prayed before his betrayal and crucifixion, ". . . Not as I will, but as Thou wilt" (Matthew 26:39), he was not eliminating or discounting his own will. In fact, he directly asked his heavenly Father to grant his desire, saying, "My Father, if it is possible, let this cup pass from Me . . . " (Matthew 26:39). That is, Jesus asked the Father to spare him from having to go through the crucifixion if there were another way to solve our sin problem.

Jesus also recognized that his wishes might differ from his Father's, and in that case he was willing to defer to the Father. Jesus exercised his own fully functioning, unique self that was separate from God the Father's self, yet Jesus never sinned. In a similar way, even when God finishes perfecting us, each of us will still be a distinct, unique individual with his or her own mind, emotions, and will.

The Apostle Paul explained the goodness of the individuality of each self by describing "the body of Christ" in 1 Corinthians 12. In his illustration, Christ is the head and Christians are the other parts of the body. One person is a foot, another is a hand, and so on. Paul says we are united yet separate. We are "members of one another," but "individually" each members of the body, connected to Christ and other Christians. We belong.

In addition, each individual is different from Christ and other Christians in ways that enable the individual to have something unique to offer. A foot is not a hand, and it is also not the head. As much as we will become like Christ through God's power, we will never *be* Christ or have our inner selves replaced by Christ. God does not call the Christian to give up his or her unique self, but to purify it from sin and allow God to develop it to maturity.

Should we die to self? Only to the old sinful self. God seeks not to destroy the mind, will, and emotions, but to fulfill all our capacities. After all, who created us?

## Summing It Up

Are we worthy of God's loving approval? Yes, when we receive worthiness as Jesus' gift to us! When we do, God credits us as with the righteousness of Jesus, so that we will never have to experience God's wrath. Our sins—past, present, and future—are forgiven.

God has placed into each of us who believes a new heart, a new moral bent that revels in goodness. Since our worthiness no longer depends on our own unpredictable performance, but on what Jesus accomplished on the cross, it is ours forever—no matter what.

Our sin no longer hinders our worthiness. Jesus has saved us from that. God, who knows all about our sin, loves us. We, too, can face our sin and experience our worth at the same time.

Despite the presence of sin, we are not cut off from experiencing to the full what God made us to be as his images. The solution is not to die to the whole self, but to transform it morally and to fulfill its God-created potential. As we cooperate with him, the Holy Spirit enables us to fulfill the potential of our capacities competently.

**Target Questions**

1. First John 1:8-9 says the following:

> *If we say that we have no sin, we are deceiving ourselves, and the truth is not in us. If we confess our sins, He is faithful and righteous to forgive us our sins and to cleanse us from all unrighteousness.*

Do you agree or disagree? Have you ever confessed to God that you are a sinner and received his forgiveness? If not, is there any reason why you would not like to do so now?

2. Which of the following do you believe makes you worthy of God's love and acceptance?

    A. My own degree of holiness or goodness.

    B. Nothing. I am unworthy.

    C. Jesus took the punishment in full for my unworthy deeds, God credits Jesus' moral perfection to my account, and God gave me a new self that longs to be as good as Jesus.

D. Other. (Explain.)

3. When you sin, which of the following do you believe God feels toward you?

A. Disgusted, angry, judgmental.

B. Amused, unconcerned.

C. Indifferent, too busy to notice.

D. Loving concern to help me learn.

E. Other. (Explain.)

4. If you were granted an unlimited lifetime exemption from being caught by any law enforcement agency, would you live any differently? If so, in what way? Although there would be no legal consequences, do you think there would be any other undesirable consequences of indulging in unlawful behavior? Would there be any worthwhile consequences for continuing to live lawfully?

5. Do you have a favorite sin? Do you ever envy people whose moral values allow them to sin? According to your understanding of Scripture, do you believe that such feelings belong to your "old self" or "sin nature"? What do you believe God would like you to do about this part of your self?

6. Are there parts of your inner self that you do not admire? How difficult is it for you to admit this? Do you think your faults affect how much God loves you?

7. Are there some godly, moral, wholesome individuals whom you admire? Does goodness appeal to you? Do you believe the longing to be good is related to your "new self"? According to your understanding of Scripture, what does God want you to do with this part of yourself? (E.g., die to it? Or nourish it in some way?)

8. After noticing you have an attitude that is sinful, what should you do?

   A. Ignore it and hope it goes away.

   B. Deny it. Insist it never happened in the first place.

   C. Try to shut off your own mind so Christ's thoughts can flow through you.

   D. Admit your sin and transform your mind by seeking to understand God's point of view and changing your sinful attitude.

9. What does the phrase, "dying to self," communicate to you? In your opinion, is it a desirable thing to do?

10. The Apostle Paul urges, "Do not be conformed to this world, but be transformed by the renewing of your mind . . ." (Romans 12:2). Do you feel you are actively engaged in this process? If not, what is getting in your way? If so, how are you going about it?

# 6
# How Can I
# Be Competent?

My most embarrassing moment occurred in a mountain cabin where, as a young camp counselor, I was conscientiously trying to cultivate a friendship with one of my junior high counselees. I had offered to help style her hair and she had accepted.

After she washed her hair, I proceeded painstakingly to wrap each lock on my own curlers. Then came the delicate comb-out. The result was definitely curls, but they were fragile. Since it was starting to rain, I knew I had to try to keep them in place. My solution was to inundate her hair with my hair spray—on top, underneath, and sideways.

Only at the end did I realize my mistake—I had accidentally used a can of deodorant. I gasped, then broke into uncontrollable laughter. The girl became quite alarmed and insisted on knowing what was wrong. With supreme effort I spit the words out through my laughter, "I used deodorant on you!" By dinnertime, the rumor had taken on a life of its own. The talk about camp was that a girl had used deodorant on her hair and hair spray on her armpits!

The inappropriateness of using deodorant for hair spray is obvious. However, many people approach their self-esteem in much the same way. They use the wrong ingredients, attempting to make competence, rather than belongingness and worthiness, the basis for a good self-image.

The reason competence is not a secure foundation for self-esteem is fairly obvious. Today my performance may be great, but what about tomorrow? Our competence depends on our performance, which is subject to change. Taken alone or primarily, competence thus does not provide secure self-esteem.

On the other hand, belongingness and worthiness based on what God has done provide the secure foundation. They cannot be taken away. Belongingness and worthiness are ours unconditionally. Accordingly, if our self-value is first settled by unchangeables, we are then free to develop competence and enjoy the process. This way, our self-esteem is not at stake. A source of anxiety is removed from our efforts to develop competence.

In the previous chapters, we have seen that we are worthy because Jesus forgives us, and we belong because God fathers us. These two principles are the cake of self-esteem; competence is the icing. The cake is the basic item, and the icing makes it better. However, icing alone does not make a cake. First things must be taken first. Competence does not work as a basis for self-esteem. It simply *enhances* a good self-image that is already in place.

When the Scriptures talk about competence, probably the majority of the time they are referring to spiritual competence—becoming like Christ or restoring the image of Christ that sin has marred. The Scriptures say that grace precedes good works, or that worthiness precedes spiritual competence, and that is how competence works in other areas as well. We settle our value and then become competent.

In Ephesians 2:8-9, Paul says, "For by grace you have been saved through faith; and that not of yourselves, it is the gift of God; not as a result of [good] works, that no one should boast." Worthiness comes first. Then in the next verse, Paul adds, "For we are His workmanship, created in Christ Jesus for good works." God planned that competence should follow worthiness and belongingness, though we often turn this order around.

I once had a client who had been actively attempting to

place belongingness and worthiness before competence. As a result, she had enjoyed the comfort and peace of healthy self-esteem. Then she entered a new profession where she met unusually glamorous people, and her self-esteem began to crumble. She began to believe she had to compete with these people on their terms in order to be as competent and glamorous as they were. She wanted to be like them, basing her self-worth on competence and competition as they did. My response to her was "Look, you have the real McCoy. Don't imitate *them*. The next time you are with them, enjoy the confidence of your worth that you already have. Let them scratch *their* heads and try to figure out how *you* do it."

## The Vision of Competence

Not basing our self-esteem primarily upon competence does not lessen the importance of our need for competence. God called humankind to rule the earth, and that means a call to competence. This competence appears to have a twofold nature: maturation of character and mastery of skills.

To rule creation for God in the exalted manner he intends, we must be holy and exercise both our natural and spiritual capabilities. The more we develop our competencies, the more we can fulfill God's wonderful vision for us as rulers.

The author of Hebrews describes this vision by quoting an ancient translation[1] of Psalm 8:4-6:

> *But one has testified somewhere, saying, "What is man, that Thou rememberest him? Or the son of man, that Thou are concerned about him? Thou hast made him for a little while lower than the angels; Thou hast crowned him with glory and honor, and hast appointed him over the works of thy hands; Thou hast put all things in subjection under his feet."* (Hebrews 2:6-8)

This passage clearly states that God has made us humans, for a little while, lower than the angels until believers reign with Christ. The implication is that God had a plan of development as a part of his purpose for humankind. That is, God had intended unfallen man to develop the unfallen creation.[2] For "a little while," man's dominion would be restricted so that man could learn what his dominion meant. His sphere would be limited to one tiny planet amidst the billions of galaxies. He would be confined to a limited physical body that would one day be changed to what can only be described as an "imperishable," glorious, powerful, "spiritual," "heavenly" body (1 Corinthians 15:42-49).

To emphasize and expand the scope of man's destined rulership, the writer of Hebrews adds, "For in subjecting all things to him, He left nothing that is not subject to him" (Hebrews 2:8). This vast and tremendous vision includes the illimitable reaches of space and whatever lies beyond that, although the realization of this vision often seems frustrated.

This passage also describes "man's present state of futility," according to Ray Stedman:

> As it is, we do not yet see everything in subjection to him. *There is the whole story of human history in a nutshell. . . . Man attempts to exercise his dominion but he no longer can do so adequately. He has never forgotten the position God gave him, for throughout the history of the race there is a continual restatement of the dreams of man for dominion over the earth and the universe. This is why we cannot keep off the highest mountain. . . . We have to get out into space. Why? Because it is there.*
>
> *Man consistently manifests a remarkable racial memory, a vestigial recollection of what God told him to do.*[3]

On the one hand, man wants to rule; on the other hand, through the rebellion of sin, man has derailed his success in God's program of developing human lordship. However, Christ has made himself to be our way back when we accept God's forgiveness and place ourselves under God's divine lordship. Then we become fellow-heirs with Christ of the inheritance that God the Father has for us — to be seated with

Christ at the right hand of the Father's own seat of rule and power. We will rule and reign with Christ, as Paul reveals in Ephesians 1:22-23 and 2:6-7:

> *And He put all things in subjection under His feet, and gave Him as head over all things to the church, which is His body, the fulness of Him who fills all in all. . . . And raised us up with Him, and seated us with Him in the heavenly places, in Christ Jesus, in order that in the ages to come He might show the surpassing riches of His grace in kindness toward us in Christ Jesus.*

The same vision of eternal rulership is foretold to us by the writer of Revelation 22:3-5, where Christ is referred to as "the Lamb":

> *And there shall no longer be any curse; and the throne of God and of the Lamb shall be in it, and His bond-servants shall serve Him; and they shall see His face, and His name shall be on their foreheads.*
> *And there shall no longer be any night; and they shall not have need of the light of a lamp nor the light of the sun, because the Lord God shall illumine them; and they shall reign forever and ever.*

From these verses we can infer that, to be eligible to fulfill all that it means to reign now and forever, certain qualifications must be met. First, as is already the case, one must be made in the image of God. God the Father met this requirement for us. Second, we must accept Jesus' solution to the problem of sin that would otherwise eliminate our moral worthiness and ability to desire or obtain a relationship with God. Third, we must get on with the development of our ability to exercise dominion in God's kingdom, both now and in the ages to come. This means cooperating with the Holy Spirit as he matures our moral character and helps us master the spiritual and natural abilities he has given us.

*Cooperation with the Holy Spirit.* We need to cooperate with the Holy Spirit, who is actualizing the glory of God's image in us. As the Holy Spirit actively restores that marred image to its intended perfection, we are no longer what we once were.

By the same token, we are not yet fully what we are going to be, because the Holy Spirit is still at work in us to actualize what we are potentially, to fulfill completely what we are as bearers of God's image. Second Corinthians 3:18 refers to this: "But we all, with unveiled face beholding as in a mirror the glory of the Lord, are being transformed into the same image from glory to glory, just as from the Lord, the Spirit." The Holy Spirit is in the process of changing us, and he will accomplish it.

What must we do in the meantime? Cooperate with him. Philippians 2:12-13 discusses both our responsibility and God's responsibility. The Apostle Paul commands us, "Work out your salvation with fear and trembling." God holds us responsible to do something. We are to be active in carrying out the changes necessary for our restoration if God's image in us is to be complete. This is our part.

There is also God's part. Paul then says, "For it is God who is at work in you, both to will and to work for *His* good pleasure." In this passage, we learn that God does not merely require us to improve ourselves by ourselves. The philosophy that says, "If it's going to be, it's up to me," does not adequately reflect God's road to competence. Nor does Paul only say, "Let go and let God." Paul says God and I each accept responsibility for my personal growth.

Why does God intend for both of us to work together? Because:
- he is infinite, and I am his finite image.
- I have life; God *is* life.
- I discover truth; God *is* truth.
- I give and receive love; God *is* love.

I am dependent on him, but he also gave me a free will. He is the source of my free will, yet he allows me to exercise it independently of him.[4] I have to cooperate with him. God does not violate or eliminate my finite personality. He works with and by means of it with cooperation from me.

## Natural Man

Of course, not everyone considers the Holy Spirit to be a necessary component in developing personal competency.

Secular man tries to attain competence through human effort and cleverness alone, and history certainly attests that amazing achievements have been accomplished in this manner. How can this be? Because the image of God, by the very nature in which God created it, has many built-in capacities: intelligence, feelings, emotions, physical power. When taken alone, these factors compose what the Bible recognizes as "natural man" (1 Corinthians 2:14). A natural man is one who uses the capacities of the image of God apart from the enlightenment, direction, or empowering of the Holy Spirit.

This approach to mastery of character and skills was brazenly expressed by William Ernest Henley in his poem "Invictus," which boasts,

> *It matters not how straight the gate,*
>     *How charged with punishment the scroll,*
> *I am the master of my fate:*
>     *I am the captain of my soul.*[5]

Henley expressed a very rebellious attitude of not caring whether God would hold him responsible for refusing to enter the narrow gate to God's kingdom. He preferred a self-willed and self-made life separated from God over a life in collaboration with the Creator.

Natural man is like a cut flower, separated from the source of life that produced him, but unlike that same flower, he is still sustained by the God who made him. Though he may still have beauty, he goes the way of spiritual death, never allowing his spiritual potential to live so that even his natural abilities may come to fuller bloom. Natural man partakes of

God-given potential without recognizing or thanking the Giver. He may affirm the nobility of man, but denies the majesty of God, who is even greater. Hence, the natural man glorifies the creature above the Creator (Romans 1:21-23). His vision is nearsighted, since he considers only the present created world. He has no idea that ultimate fulfillment comes from loving, and cooperating with, God.

**Passive Faith**
Cooperating with the Holy Spirit is accomplished through both passive and active faith – that is, by letting the Holy Spirit do his work in us and by our working alongside him also. Let's look at passive faith first.

An advertisement for Gloria Vanderbilt perfume entices us with the words "Let it release the splendor of you." The Scriptures say *we*, not an artificial substance, are the sweet fragrance of Christ (2 Corinthians 2:14-16). The grandest beauty and splendor a human being can hope for is to be completely like Christ (Colossians 1:27-28), the gloriously perfect image of God (2 Corinthians 3:18). We have this potential through the power of the Holy Spirit, whom we should permit to release our splendor.

Allowing the Holy Spirit to "release our splendor" is what I would like to call passive faith. Our primary model for passive faith is Jesus himself. Even Jesus did not merely live under his own initiative and power, but was led and empowered by his Father, who lived in him. Jesus said, "Do you not believe that I am in the Father, and the Father is in Me? The words that I say to you I do not speak on My own initiative, but the Father abiding in Me does His works" (John 14:10). Likewise, Jesus explained, we must allow him to live in us, and we must rely on him for our source of spiritual competence: "Abide in Me, and I in you. As the branch cannot bear fruit of itself, unless it abides in the vine, so neither can you, unless you abide in Me. I am the vine, you are the branches; he who abides in Me, and I in him; he bears much fruit; for apart from Me you can do nothing" (John 15:4-5).

We abide in Christ as we draw upon his Spirit. Jesus said that although he was returning to heaven, he would live in his followers by means of the Holy Spirit, the "Helper":

> *But I tell you the truth, it is to your advantage that I go away; for if I do not go away, the Helper shall not come to you; but if I go, I will send Him to you. . . .*
>
> *But when He, the Spirit of truth, comes, He will guide you into all the truth; for He will not speak on His own initiative, but whatever He hears, He will speak; and He will disclose to you what is to come.*
>
> *He shall glorify Me; for He shall take of Mine, and shall disclose it to you. All things that the Father has are Mine; therefore I said, that He takes of Mine, and will disclose it to you.* (John 16:7, 13-15)

Jesus' point is that we should be led and empowered by the Holy Spirit just as he was by his Father. We are to trust God and submit to his work in us.

One day a man stood on the edge of a cliff overlooking the ocean. He was preparing himself to take off into the wind with a hang glider. His body was in a vertical position but his glider rested horizontally above him. As long as the man and the glider were in this perpendicular position, he got nowhere. However, when the glider filled with air, it lifted him off the cliff and carried him wherever he directed it, as he utilized the power of the air currents.

In a similar manner, the Scriptures liken the work of the Holy Spirit to invisible but powerful wind (John 3:8 and Acts 2:2-4). When we line ourselves up with the Holy Spirit's work in us, we have the very power of God changing us so that we can fulfill all God meant us to be and do.

*Steps of Faith.* It has not always been easy for me to trust in God. While chatting with a small group of committed Christian friends at church one Sunday, I admitted that I had difficulty believing God would show himself powerful in re-

101

sponse to my prayers. Sure, I believed prayer served a purpose—to help me focus on God and express my love to him, to reflect on my life and sort out my thinking from his viewpoint, to consider what could be God's good purpose in allowing a particular trial, to think of possible godly solutions to try. But did I believe God would actually intervene in events as I requested? No. This was my confession. I was not proud of my lack of faith. In fact, I was very saddened by it. But there it was.

Others in our circle that day admitted to the same weak faith. Honesty reigned. Only one said he usually believed. I prayed, asking God to help me.

A few weeks later, a friend kept coming to mind, someone who I knew was struggling with a very grave sin. I had never before believed God could help a person overcome that particular problem. But that weekend, I had an unusual spiritual experience. Faith poured over me. I felt compelled to pray earnestly over an entire weekend for God to heal this person. Then the urgency lifted and I had peace regarding my friend. Several days later, I learned that he had undergone a storm of temptation that had ended in his deciding, for the first time, that he wanted to give up any option of acting on his temptation and that he wished to pursue God's healing process.

In passive faith, I had waited for God to work in me. He did. However, as is so often the case, passive faith resulted in active faith—the faith to take action, for example, to pray—believing that God frequently desires responsive action and will use it.

### Active Faith

God expects us to develop the abilities he created within us. It is only when we use these without depending on God that we are in the wrong. Then we are what the Scriptures call "natural man" who lives "in the flesh" or according to the old sin nature (for example, 1 Corinthians 2:14–3:3).

Even taken on their own, natural abilities in themselves are God-given and good. Genesis 1:31 tells us, "And God saw all that He had made, and behold, it was very good." The abilities to reason, use language, feel, decide/choose, evaluate ourselves, relate to God, and exercise physical strength and the like are all good.

Any of these abilities can, nevertheless, be misused. That is why some Christians tend to be suspicious of them altogether. Have you heard such comments as "Don't try to reason out God's ways" or "Don't use your feelings" or "Break the will"? Christians who say such things often-times have unfortunately equated our human abilities with the flesh.

Some Christian groups, for example, stress right doctrine and behavior while warning against the use of emotions in the Christian life. Others may emphasize feeling love and praise for God and meaningfully experiencing immediate contact with God and people, but simultaneously neglect Bible scholarship.

The Scriptures indicate, however, that we have truly mastered godliness when our *whole* being is actively functioning and embracing what is right. Jesus commanded, " 'You shall love the Lord your God with all your heart, and with all your soul, and with all your mind' " (Matthew 22:37). He said that when we do this and also love our neighbors as ourselves, we have mastered the inner qualities of godliness totally. Only to the degree that we love God's ways with the mind, emotions, and will, all three, have we truly begun to master spiritual competence.

As a young adult, I remember agreeing with God's laws of morality only in my behavior. In my heart, I envied those who sinned. My emotions were a vital cue that my need for logical understanding needed to be satisfied. As I, in faith, sought reasons why God's way is best, I grew in love for him and his ways with my mind and emotions, too.

In the process, I exercised *passive faith* by believing God would give me understanding, and I also used *active faith* by studying God's Word and observing people's experiences – all the while trusting that God would be guiding and helping me. I activated my mind, emotions, and faith – the natural and spiritual capacities God created. God used my active faith.

As it is with maturation of character, so it is also with mastery of skills: we must apply faith that acts. Our God-given abilities grow as we use them. Though God created our built-in capacities, they still need to be cultivated.

Diligence in this area is necessary. Paul admonishes us to be "not lagging behind in diligence, fervent in spirit, serving the Lord" (Romans 12:11). As God reveals our gifts, we must use them. The more we use them, the more we see what our gifts can do, and that perception helps us grow in confidence and faith.

A young man who was learning this truth believed God wanted him to prepare for some type of full-time ministry. He thought he should go to seminary, but felt he lacked sufficient writing skills for the task. Nevertheless, he decided to exercise active faith by stepping out to apply himself to what he could do, all the while also exercising passive faith, trusting God to work out the rest. The young man accepted a position overseeing the construction of a scientific station in Antarctica where he had worked several years before.

As soon as he set foot off the ski-equipped plane in Antarctica, his boss greeted him and gave him a warm office and a request for a status report on the progress of the construction already underway. These reports were required daily. At first, they were an awful grind for the young man, but after several weeks, the task seemed less bothersome. His writing ability was gradually improving.

It finally dawned on him that he was becoming skilled as a writer! God had guided him to a place where he was forced to write on a subject that interested him and in which he had considerable expertise. Not only that, he had a supportive boss who provided encouragement and coaching. He had found himself in a perfect position to improve his writing.

Upon returning to the United States, he enrolled in a seminary.

This young man had had the passive faith to trust the Holy Spirit to intervene, and he had exercised the active faith to get himself moving. He became competent as he cooperated with the Holy Spirit.

**Summing It Up**
We have seen that competence (maturation of character and mastery of skills) can best be founded on faith – dependency on, and trust in, God. Dependence upon God comes in two forms – the passive and the active. The Scriptures reveal that the way to competence requires both. Through passive faith, we are led and empowered by the Holy Spirit. By active faith, we walk in his direction and power.

The next chapter has more to say about developing competence.

**Target Questions**

1. Which of the following statements best expresses your view of the most effective way to become competent?

    A. If it's going to be, it's up to me.

    B. Let go and let God.

    C. God has provided all the resources I need. But from here on, it's up to me and what I do with those resources.

    D. God has provided all the resources I need. As I accept the responsibility to use them actively and to the best of my present understanding, I rely on him to be working in me, too.

2. What are some personal qualities (e.g., patience, tact, assertiveness) that you would like more of? What are some

skills you would like to develop better? Do you believe the Holy Spirit will help you as you make the necessary effort?

3. Think of a time (especially recently) when you were disappointed in your maturity or skills. Did you (mark all that apply):

    A.  replay critical tapes and feel lowered self-esteem?

    B.  worry about what others would think of you?

    C.  fear some form of punishment?

    D.  remember God loves you anyway?

    E.  believe God forgives you and will help you improve?

    F.  still see yourself as God's own image?

4. Do you tend to think some people are innately more valuable than others in *God's* eyes? If so, which people? People who are more intelligent? beautiful? thin? healthy? strong? popular or famous? wealthy? capable? talented? loving? moral? powerful? church attenders? church leaders? members of a certain race? members of a particular nationality? men or women? older or younger people? yourself or others?

5. Do you *personally* tend to consider some people more valuable than others? If so, again, which people?

6. If you tend to consider some people less valuable in your eyes or God's, consider these questions about such people:

    A.  Are they the images of God as truly as you are?

    B.  Is God able to forgive them and make them worthy? Does he love them whether they have repented of their sin or not?

    C.  Can they develop their God-created capabilities by cooperating with the Holy Spirit?

7. Pray that God will help you develop competence. He has gifted you with the skills to do so and will enable you to change any attitudes that may hinder you.

# 7
# HOW CAN I BECOME THE REAL ME?

A woman used to buy secondhand furniture, refinish it, and sell it in order to donate the proceeds to missions. One day while scouting for items at a garage sale, the man of the house invited her to rummage through his shed full of discarded, dust-smothered pieces of furniture. He apparently preferred more modern furniture and wished to be rid of the old. The woman bought two nightstands and a wardrobe for about one-hundred-fifty dollars each.

Suspecting that their true value was greater than the former owner had realized, she took the pieces to an antique appraiser. Her suspicions were confirmed. The furniture had originated in Europe in the 1800s and had possibly been used in a monastery. All three pieces were in excellent condition and had the original patina. What was their full value? She sold the pair of nightstands for nine hundred dollars and the wardrobe for eleven hundred dollars. Their appraised market value was even higher!

The original owner had not known the value of what he had had or its potential. Making the effort to learn its true nature would have profited him far beyond his meager dreams. The furniture he sold was likely worth much more than its more modern replacements.

In a similar manner, God wants us to discover who we are and what our unique potential is. As we do so, we will let him accomplish through our lives far more than we would otherwise ask or think. If we do not recognize and value our God-given potential, we might set it aside or attempt to replace it by imitating someone else's personality. God wishes us to become who we are.

## A Special Name

George MacDonald, a writer who deeply influenced C. S. Lewis, was keenly aware of God's concern for our indentity. MacDonald found explicit reference to this concern in Revelation 2:17, where we read:

> He who has an ear, let him hear what the Spirit says to the churches. To him who overcomes, to him I will give some of the hidden manna, and I will give him a white stone, and a new name written on the stone which no one knows but he who receives it.

In the Scriptures, a person's name typically stands for the very nature or fundamental character of the person. It is the word that sums up the individual. The Scriptures say that one day God will bestow on each Christian a new name that only the receiver and the Giver will know, the name that expresses who the believer was designed to be in the mind of God.

Each person was created to be a unique version of the image of God. MacDonald suggests that God wants the believer to discern his or her special significance in God's plan and to fulfill it.[1] When this task is completed, the name is conferred as a reward to say, "You are now what your name means. Well done, thou good and faithful servant. Enter into the joy of thy Lord and reign with Me."

As we recognize who we are in the mind of God and are in the process of becoming that, we will realize our true potential and achieve competence in both maturation of character and mastery of skills. Unfortunately, we may sidetrack ourselves from our goal by focusing on how we compare to others and by trying to be what they are.

## Comparing Ourselves

A pastor prayed one day, "Lord, enable me to preach like Pastor X. He is so eloquent!" Immediately, he felt as though the Lord spoke back to him, "I don't want you to be another Pastor X. I've had enough trouble with him already!" The praying pastor decided to develop his own style of preaching.

One of the clearest passages in Scripture about individual differences is 1 Corinthians 12. While Revelation 2:17 seems to address the uniqueness of the total individual, 1 Corinthians 12 focuses specifically on spiritual gifts with a principle that can have very broad application.

Here the Apostle Paul reveals that the Holy Spirit has conferred spiritual competencies or gifts on every Christian, and he assigns them to each believer as he himself chooses. Each person is gifted to be a different part of Christ's body of believers.

The Spirit of God does not endow everyone with the same competencies. He bestows them "as *he* wills" (1 Corinthians 12:11, 18). A person who is a "helper" should not conclude, "I'm not a leader; therefore I'm a zero. My abilities don't count because they aren't like so-and-so's." Yes, we may be tempted to evaluate our capabilities by comparing them to someone else's. However, Paul is teaching that each person should compare what he or she is being and doing to what God has gifted and called that individual to be and to do. In other words, compare yourself to yourself. Success is always possible by that standard.

If we measure ourselves by other people, there will always be somebody who will exceed us in some area. If we have to outdo others to have value, then only one person can win self-esteem, namely God. God alone will never be surpassed by anyone.

How much wiser it is to compare our achievements to our own God-given potential. In other words, be what you are. No one can do that as well as you can. This principle makes sense when applied to other abilities beside spiritual gifts, too.

111

No one can do everything well. Some think that having a positive self-image requires believing that we perform masterfully at everything and never admitting we do poorly at anything. How unrealistic!

One night in a group therapy session, a woman lamented, "When I was a teenager, I used to have so much confidence. I thought I could do anything! I don't feel that way anymore. What's happened to me?" Another person spontaneously blurted out, "Your judgment has improved!" The group howled with laughter. Actually, this person had not intended the comment as a putdown but as a compliment. No one can do everything well, and realistic acceptance of our strengths and weaknesses comes with maturity.

If we are secure in our worth, we need not excel at everything in order to feel competent. Rather, we can accept our abilities and limits realistically. "That's me, and that's good enough," we will believe. We will enjoy flexing our own capability muscles without having to be more or less than we can be.

Accepting our limitations is not meant to restrict us from discovering new potentials. It is to help us see our worth within the limitations of our finiteness. The point is to prevent us from basing our value on how we compare to others. Each believer is set apart to be a unique member of Christ's body, to do his or her part in God's kingdom.

Comparing ourselves to others who are more able can lead to deflated self-esteem, but it can also result in an inflated ego, or pride, if we compare better (1 Corinthians 12:21-25; 2 Corinthians 1:12-13, 24; Romans 12:3-5).

The Apostle Paul recommends we use sound judgment (Romans 12:3) in assessing our gifts, strengths, potential, and abilities. Accepting an accurate self-estimate of our "givens" is biblical humility. True humility is neither self-effacing nor egotistical. We are thus not really being humble if we have an inaccurately lower opinion of ourselves. At the other extreme, we should not overestimate ourselves, either. How high an estimate of one's own competence can a person have and still use sound judgment? In Paul's case, at least, very high.[2] He said, "I exhort you, therefore, be imitators of me" (1 Corinthians 4:16). Humility is not necessarily having a low self-image, but an accurate one.

It is only when we use our self-estimates to claim superior personal worth or more credit than we deserve that we are boasting. Muhammad Ali, world champion of boxing, proclaimed, "I am the greatest!" Was he trying to elevate his value above that of others? Did he mean he deserved all the credit, or did he give God the glory due to him, too? I cannot judge.

The first-century Christians at Corinth were having a problem with bragging. Paul corrected them by asking some pointed questions: "For who regards you as superior? And what do you have that you did not receive? But if you did receive it, why do you boast as if you had not received it?" (1 Corinthians 4:7).

If our competencies glorify God, it is because God gifted us and the Holy Spirit led and empowered us. Taken alone, our effort, obedience, and self-discipline — as important as they are — would never have been enough. We had nothing to do with God's choice to gift us.

If we have been specially endowed, it is so that we may give. We must trust God to help others through us, and then we need to step out in faith. As God works through our faithfulness our competency can grow, and we enhance our already good self-image. However we must remember to give God the credit and praise for his gifts, never using them to compete with others for personal value.

The purpose of our God-given abilities — whether they be spiritual gifts or natural abilities — is for us to nourish one another's competencies so that we can collectively reach the world for Christ's kingdom (Ephesians 4:16; 1 Corinthians 12:7). How can we generously help one another develop competency if we insist upon competing instead of cooperating? When the parts of a body turn against each other, that body becomes diseased and ineffective. As members of Christ's body, we can best develop our competencies as we help one another develop under the headship of Christ and the empowering of the Holy Spirit, who has gifted us in the first place. The members of Christ's body must be team players, not prima donnas.

## Beyond Striving

I once overheard a Sunday school teacher at a large church say, "I'm going to be the best teacher in our Sunday school." Inspiration "to be the best for God" leads to endless striving.

As Brownback points out, Saul was head and shoulders above the people, but then he met Goliath who was head and shoulders above himself. "There is always the need to keep climbing, always the fear that Goliath will come along. For the president there is always another election."[3] For the Olympic gold medalist, there are younger ranks of succeeding athletes.

We will never finally be the best. Only God is. Even if we do set world records, someone will one day break our records and pass us up. Don't worry about being *the* best. Be *your* best.

Comparison to others is the quickest route to feelings of inferiority or superiority. Don't measure your performance by comparison to others. Compare your level of competency to your own God-given potentials as you discover them.

As you do this, your feelings of competency can remain strong despite any shortcomings or failures you may experience while growing and learning to be who you can be. Use setbacks to help you learn and grow.

## Fear of Failure

A young woman purposely allowed herself to lose games for her varsity tennis team for no reason she could understand. She discovered her critical tape told her she must be the best in order to accept herself at all. Anything less was failure. Her motto was "Better not to try and never truly to test whether I'm the best than to risk discovering I might not be!" For her, failure itself was her way of avoiding failure.

One of the biggest obstacles to achieving competency is fear of failure. "I can't do it" is a self-defeating attitude that interferes with putting forth wholehearted effort.

Failure sometimes reveals an area where our potential is limited or weak. It does not necessarily mean "I can never do it." The only thing a failure shows for certain is that we didn't do it that time and need to try again. We are all entitled to our quota of failures. David, as a shepherd boy, understood this.

Do you remember how David slew Goliath? David was the only one who believed God would conquer this giant. Before fatally wounding God's enemy, David's faith enabled him to say, "This day the Lord will deliver you up into my hands" (1 Samuel 17:46). Nevertheless, before attacking, David gathered not one, but five, smooth stones for his slingshot. He did not know how many tries it might take. He might fail before succeeding.

This prospect of failure as part of the route to success was so taken for granted that David matter-of-factly included it in his strategy.[4] And this was true despite the fact that David had enjoyed past successes in active faith. He said, "Your servant has killed both the lion and the bear. . . . The Lord who delivered me from the paw of the lion and from the paw of the bear, He will deliver me from the hand of this Philistine" (1 Samuel 17:36-37).

**Winners versus Losers**
The difference between winners and losers is that winners learn from their failures, but losers give up. Losers use setbacks as evidence to "prove" they are inadequate human beings. They lower their self-esteem and discourage themselves. Winners use failures to collect data on how to do something better in the future, and in so doing, they reassure themselves of their potential. The road to competence is paved with the less-than-competent experiences of the past.

Madam Marie Curie, a French physicist and twice Nobel Prize winner, is known today for the work she did with her husband and later on her own after his death. In 1898, Pierre and Marie Curie announced to the world that they had discovered polonium and radium in pitchblende. However, it took them four years of trial and error to discover how to isolate radium in its pure form. During those years, they suffered financial hardship and could have given up. Instead, they loved their work and fulfilled their God-given potential.

How fortunate for us that they persevered. Following their triumph, they freely gave to the world their process for obtaining radium without any thought to their own gain. Madame Curie's daughter wrote of her, "She had . . . an immense religious respect for human life."[5] Many people have been blessed by their achievements because radium has been used in the treatment of cancer and other diseases. Many failures eventually led to their final successes.

The more our self-esteem is settled before we pursue competence, the less failure will wound us. When I left my employment in a larger clinic and launched into independent private practice, I consciously divorced my self-esteem from the idea of success. This was a good thing, because the first several months, my client load dropped. I was depressed and longed for the circumstances I had left behind.

"What if I eventually have to go to a colleague for a job?" I wondered. If I failed, I believed I would be the first to admit, "I gave it a good try; it didn't work out." During this time I never attacked my value or potential. When the practice did succeed, I felt confident that I had the business administration skills needed for my independent practice as a psychologist. This both enhanced the good self-esteem I already had and increased my faith in what God could do as well.

**Fear of Success – Fear of Pride**
While some people fear failure, others fear success. Obviously, either can hinder developing competence.

At a committee meeting, a woman was flooded with verbal garlands of commendation by her boss. Her fellow employees awkwardly sat around the conference table with her as their boss extolled her apparently goddesslike attributes to the heights. The embarrassed woman wanted to hide under the table. After the meeting, one of her coworkers impishly inquired, "What is it like to be truly wonderful?"

Different people have varying feelings about personal glory, but most of us probably experience some mixture of feeling both rewarded and uncomfortable. We may be struggling between enjoying the enhancement of our self-esteem and not wanting to feel pride. How can we feel successful and humble at the same time?

Robert Schuller, in his book *Self-Esteem: The New Reformation*, makes an interesting statement about achievement and personal glory:

> By self-denial we cannot accept that Christ is calling us to a dishonest and demeaning humility. I have no doubt that millions, yes multiplied millions of God-given, self-esteem-generating dreams and ideas have been sent by God's Holy Spirit into Christian minds who forthrightly rejected them — for one reason . . . the idea immediately promised ego fulfillment. Poor misguided, sincere Christian souls, sensing the birth of noble self-esteem as they image the development of this dream, told themselves, "This must be pride. It must be my will, and that means it cannot be God's will." God's biggest problem is to motivate us to accept his divine dreams even if they hold the prospect of ego-fulfillment. God's dreams always hold the promise of self-esteem satisfaction. We need not, however, fear that we shall be "guilty of going off on an ego trip" if we pursue those divine ideas that hint at the possibility of some personal glory along the way. For there will be a cross before we gain the crown. And the cross will sanctify the ego trip![6]

Schuller is explaining fear of success as fear of pride. He encourages Christians to accept personal glory as a legitimate outcome of achieving God-given dreams. By saying this, Schuller has stirred up controversy. Is Schuller right?

First, I believe Schuller has described a real problem. Fear of pride has caused many Christians to fear success. However, should Christians fear pride? I think the answer depends on what we mean by pride. Pride can have more than one meaning.

## What Is Pride?

Pride can mean an attitude of:

♦ preferring myself to others
♦ superiority
♦ giving myself priority over others
♦ seeing myself as having more value than others.

This kind of pride is self-esteem based on comparing myself to other people and desiring to matter more than they do.

The Scriptures consistently show that God is against such an attitude of conceit and arrogance: "The fear of the Lord is to hate evil; pride and arrogance and the evil way, and the perverted mouth, I hate" (Proverbs 8:13).

There are other good reasons for fearing this type of pride. A superior attitude is obnoxious to others and destructive to relationships. It may harm the self-esteem of someone else who is made to feel inferior to us, inspiring others to jealousy, rivalry, and resentment.

Furthermore, as we have discussed, we cannot stay superior forever. Someone *will* pass us up. Realistically, a pompous attitude is bound to be followed by a great fall and some embarrassment, which is the opposite feeling from this kind of pride. Proverbs 16:18 reminds us that "pride goes before destruction, and a haughty spirit before stumbling." A Christian should be concerned if the motive for pursuing a dream is to be valued or preferred over others.

*Pride* can also mean:

♦ proper respect for myself
♦ a sense of my own dignity or worth.

Such pride is always accompanied by the realization that

what gives me worth gives the same worth to *all* human beings. This pride may be the conviction that I have been created in the image of God.

Pride can also mean delight or satisfaction in my achievements or in someone else's. In other words, pride can mean the wholesome self-esteem that comes from competence. It is the joy and the fulfillment that come from exercising and developing our unique, God-created potential. This type of pride will accompany success, and a Christian should not fear it. This is a feeling God will cause us to experience when he praises and honors us one day, saying, "Well done, thou good and faithful servant: thou hast been faithful over a few things, I will make thee ruler over many things: enter thou into the joy of thy lord" (Matthew 25:21, *KJV*).

Pride as self-preference is evil. Pride as self-esteem is wholesome. These different attitudes should not be confused with each other. The Apostle Paul distinguishes them in Romans 2:6-8. He refers to God,

> *Who will render to every man according to his deeds: to those who by perseverance in doing good seek for glory and honor and immortality, eternal life; but to those who are selfishly ambitious and do not obey the truth, but obey unrighteousness, wrath and indignation.*

The motivation to seek glory, honor, and immortality by perseverance and doing good is holy, but selfish ambition and disobedience to God are unrighteous. Selfish ambition results in evil of every sort.

As the Apostle James observes, "For where jealousy and selfish ambition exist, there is disorder and every evil thing" (James 3:16). However, unselfishly giving ourselves to our kingdom tasks will result in finding a full life and joy. Jesus explained, "For whoever wishes to save his life shall lose it; but whoever loses his life for My sake shall find it" (Matthew 16:25). When the Apostle Paul says, "Christ in you, the hope of glory" (Colossians 1:27), he is acknowledging our desire for glory as a legitimate one. He is also telling us how to attain it – by mastering Christ-likeness.

In the award-winning film *Chariots of Fire*, two Olympic runners win gold medals. One runner sought success in order to bolster his sagging self-esteem by becoming the best. When he succeeded, he became depressed and isolated himself, unable to celebrate his victory because it did not accomplish what he had hoped.

The other runner was a Christian who recognized the nature of the capabilities God had given him. He said, "I believe God made me for a purpose, but I believe he also made me fast. And when I run, I feel his pleasure." He sought to become all that God had made him to be in order to show how good and amazing God is. When he won, his hope was realized. God was glorified, and he was glorious, too. His face – his entire being – radiated deep satisfaction. As his fellow athletes paraded him on their shoulders before the cheering crowds in the stadium, he reveled in the joy and celebration.

The goal of fulfilling what God made us to be should free us from the fear of failure and inferiority or the fear of success and pride that comes from basing our feelings of competency on how we compare to others.

**Overachievers Anonymous**
Whenever we encourage competency, we risk driving people to overemphasize achievement to the point of neglecting their other needs, such as relaxation and relationships. Competency means fulfilling the *whole* person.

A journalist was lecturing before a group of Christian writers, including myself, on how to become successful by running from the minute our feet hit the floor in the morning until we fell into bed at night. He recommended that we find a way to turn every second into an opportunity to work and always aim to do as many things at once as possible. It was as though we should feverishly slave in a constant state of emergency. After panting through his exhausting lecture, someone privately suggested it should have been titled, "Have a Heart Attack for Jesus." Fortunately, the speaker received this "advice" in good humor.

How much striving for competency is enough? Any striving apart from faith is too much. It is the way of anxiety. Effort made in faith that the Holy Spirit will enable us allows us to have peace and contentment along the way. Faith strikes the balance between acting to accomplish more on the one hand and being content with what we have (1 Timothy 6:6-8) on the other hand.

If we overextend our investments of time, energy, or money, we may wear out or run out. When our resources are tied up in just the process of maintaining our present commitments, there are none left over with which to grow. It takes time to enjoy the fruit of past labor (Ecclesiastes 5:18), to reflect on our lives, and to dream of what God might have us do. It may take money to support God's work, to invest toward future goals, to launch a new vision. Anything we do is liable to require a reservoir of energy upon which to draw. An overachiever is like a sprinter who puts out at maximum level all the way down a short track. How much wiser to live life as a long-distance runner who paces himself and goes farther.

We must accept that God alone is infinite and we are finite. God never intended any one of us to save the whole world. That is his responsibility, and even he will not win with everyone (in the sense that not everyone will respond to him). Our jobs are to tend our own provinces in God's kingdom. In other words, each one should do his or her *part*—however big or small that may be.

If we neglect the spiritual condition of ourselves and others for whom we are directly responsible for the sake of achievement, we are lopsided, overdone in some areas at great expense to others. Then, we are probably trying to do more than God gave us time, energy, and capacity to do.

If so, it is time to check our motives. Whose kingdom are

we trying to build: God's or our own? And are we acting out of faith or insecurity? "Whatever is not from faith is sin" (Romans 14:23).

Selfish ambition (James 3:14-15) is a hard taskmaster. Often, it is the result of measuring our value by our accomplishments, which does not work. Belongingness and worthiness must come before competence. Achievement taken alone never gets us to the point that we finally settle our worth. It says, "So on to longer hours and more strenuous effort!"

By contrast, Jesus is a wonderful employer. He says, "My yoke is easy, and My load is light" (see Matthew 11:28-30). Our self-esteem is a result of grace, not something for which we labor.

If you belong to "Overachievers Anonymous," take heart. We need not sell our own souls, the quality of our lives, or the needs of those we love in the vain effort to gain the whole world (Matthew 16:26) or to achieve. The Holy Spirit, as we cooperate with him, will see to it that we become what God made each of us to be as a unique version of God's image. He will actualize our potential. Overstriving makes us pour too much of our energy into some competencies on which we erroneously base our self-esteem and too little energy into others. This is never the case with the Holy Spirit, who cultivates a fulfilled, well-rounded person.

### The Promise of Competency

God promises that our development will be completed. That fact can bring us reassurance and comfort. Because of it, the Apostle Paul was able to express the wonderful confidence that God will finish this process of restoring our competency to be like Christ. God will actualize all we are meant to be as his image.

Romans 8:29-30 promises,

> *For whom He foreknew, He also predestined* to become conformed to the image of His Son, that He might be the first-born

*among many brethren; and whom He predestined, these He also called; and whom He called, these He also justified; and whom He justified, these He also glorified.*

If Jesus makes us worthy (justifies us), then the Holy Spirit is also going to make us competent (glorify us). That is, God's Spirit is going to finish the work of renewal and cause each of us to fulfill the majesty and glory of being a unique version of the image of God in its full, restored form so that we can rule and reign with Christ. The moment of completion will be when we see Christ (1 John 3:2-3).

## Summing It Up

We become competent as we cooperate with the Holy Spirit to fulfill our unique potential. Each of us is a specially gifted, one-of-a-kind version of the image of God. If we measure our worth by how our competency compares to that of others, we will likely wind up feeling either inadequate or haughty. Wholesome self-esteem comes from being what you can be.

Since our self-esteem is based on givens from God, we can risk the failures that pave the road to success, because our own self-esteem is not at stake. We are also free to accept our realistic limitations and to avoid overstriving. Rather than fear success, we can enjoy it because it enhances our already settled self-esteem and glorifies God.

The God who bestows belongingness and worthiness will also provide us with competence. He richly lavishes upon us all we need to fulfill this self-esteem triad. We are competent as God's Spirit enables us and as we fellowship and cooperate with him. We are worthy because Jesus graciously forgives us, and we belong because God lovingly fathers us. The Apostle Paul's benediction, according to Maurice Wagner, affirms this three-pronged activity of the Triune God that we have seen is the source of our self-esteem:[7] "The grace of the Lord Jesus Christ, and the love of God, and the fellowship of the Holy Spirit, be with you all" (2 Corinthians 13:14).

Hence, let each of us cast aside our critical tapes and instead place our trust in the affirming message, "God loves me, and I am somebody." Applying the fundamentals of self-esteem will enable us to get off our own backs when we experience depression, guilt, or anger, so that we can be free to love, as the remaining chapters reveal.

## Target Questions

1. How often do you find yourself comparing your abilities with those of others for the purpose of measuring your own value? When you do this (assuming everyone does sometimes), do you struggle more with feelings of inferiority or of pride? Do these feelings satisfy your need for secure self-esteem?

2. Do you ever have fantasies of being elevated as more valuable than other people—for example, by means of having wealth, power, prestige, beauty, charm, talent, superior achievement, or fame? If so, what are your particular fantasies? Do they interfere with your motivation to devote your life to the Lord?

3. Do you have a vision for what God would like you to do as your part in his kingdom? If you were to lose your life in service to the Lord (believing this is how you would find your life), what would you be doing and what would your life-style be like? Would this kind of life give you joy? Would it involve the fullest expression of you as God made you?

4. How much do you experience fear of failure or fear of success? What do you think causes such feelings, especially in yourself? Is the cause a fear of feeling inferior or superior? Are there other feelings involved? What do you think is the cure?

5. Are you a workaholic? If so, what has it cost you? What have been the rewards? Has it been worth it? Do you want to

continue living this way? What changes, if any, would you like to make?

6.  Are you an underachiever? If so, what do you think is getting in the way of your fulfilling your potential? Can you do something about it? Do you care to change?

7.  Ask God to help you discover who you are in his design in order to become the person he will describe by a new name one day (Revelation 2:17), a person who can use his/her God-given abilities to reign with Christ forever.

8.  If you are working through this book with a study group, the following exercise may assist you in helping one another discover what your spiritual gifts and natural capabilities are.

Choose one member of the group and have each person (including the chosen member) independently write down what abilities he/she sees in the chosen member. Then read these descriptions, and allow the chosen member to ask questions or comment upon this feedback. How does the chosen member's self-description compare with the views expressed by others?

Repeat this procedure, allowing each group member who so desires to be the chosen member and receive this type of feedback.

If you are discussing this chapter with a study group, have the group close with this prayer:

> *Father, we come to you, each of us a unique version of your image reflecting some facet of you. Empower us, by your Spirit, to enter into that facet of you in order that we may know, understand, and, as priests, express that part of you to our brothers and sisters. Amen.*

# 8
# IS MY DEPRESSION NORMAL?

Have you ever had experiences like these?

♦ Your boss warns you that you are not making the grade. This is the third job where you have failed. You just learned your husband is having an affair. Someone in your family is struggling with alcoholism, homosexuality, or mental illness.

♦ The dearest person in all the world, your beloved and most precious one, announces that the relationship is to be no more. Your dream is now a nightmare.

♦ Your estranged spouse is fighting you for the custody of your children. Or you are a single parent who is fighting to support your children and yourself emotionally and financially. You cannot find the time, money, or energy for legal means to collect unpaid child support.

♦ Your baby died. The funeral was six weeks ago. Everyone has forgotten that your grief is not over.

♦ Your child has learning disabilities. His overworked teachers do not seem to have the patience to give him special understanding. No treatment has helped. He watches his sister excel. You see him rebel.

♦ Your unmarried daughter is pregnant or just had an abortion. She pushes away your caring and advice.

♦ Your son turns on you. He wants revenge for all the times he feels you did not understand. When he still is not home at 3:00 A.M., you wonder if he is injured or in jail.

♦ The doctors say you will never walk again. Your physical pain will be constant. The career for which you have prepared will never be.

♦ You are invited to share your prayer requests in church. Inside your head, a loud clashing din echos, "I can't tell that!" You are alone with your secret pain. You wonder, "Whom can I tell?" For the hundredth time, you mentally file through everyone you know. No one seems quite right. At night, you cry till your throat aches. You feel so empty. Is there no hope? No end?

♦ You have been in the crucible of pain so long that sometimes along the way you have sinned and thereby worsened your condition and grieved yourself. That is part of your suffering, too.

"Is God still there?" you cry out. "Why is he letting this happen to me? Is this how he shows the world he is alive and active in his children? Why doesn't he do something! Will he punish me for being mad at him?

"Is it all my fault? If I had enough faith and were more mature, this would not depress me. I should be rising above this. Is this 'the joy of the Lord'?"

If you have experienced depression from circumstances such as those just described and wondered if your feelings were OK, this chapter is for you.

**What Is Depression?**
Depression is a mood disturbance, a reaction to loss, threatened loss, failure, discouragement, or disillusionment. It is feeling "blue," "down," or "sad."

This feeling can occur in varying degrees and for varying lengths of time. The spectrum of this emotion includes anything from a "sinking" feeling that lasts but a moment to agony so deep and long-lasting that you wonder if you will ever feel joy again.

Sometimes life deals us hard blows, and it often seems that

"when it rains, it pours." I recall sliding down a mountainside on a metal saucer one day as a teenager and then being abruptly thrown into the air and pounded into the ground. All the air was knocked out of my lungs. As I gasped with all my might to suck in one single breath of air, wondering whether I was about to die, my friends behind me, who could not see me struggling for my very survival, were laughing. I have often thought that life can be like that experience. As soon as you begin to get that first breath, something knocks you down again and again and again. No wonder people may succumb to depression.

Besides affecting the mood, depression may be accompanied by physical symptoms, such as:
♦ insomnia
♦ change in appetite
♦ loss of sexual interest.

David experienced depression, which he aptly expressed in the Book of Psalms. When we are feeling down, we may be able to identify with his feelings. In Psalm 6, he says, "My bones are dismayed . . . my soul is greatly dismayed. . . ."

We see both emotional and physical sensations in David's expression of depression:

> I am weary with my sighing;
> Every night I make my bed swim,
> I dissolve my couch with my tears.
> My eye has wasted away with grief;
> It has become old because of all my adversaries. (vv. 6-7)

He felt physically dull and old because he was so discouraged and drained. David's depression was a normal reaction to prolonged threat by his enemies upon his life. He was not mentally ill. He just felt down.

Depression may be normal or abnormal. *Normal depression* is simply a response to the types of circumstances described above. (One technical psychological term for normal depression is "reactive depression.")

*Abnormal depression* occurs when there is an additional factor, namely that the person's self-critical tapes begin to replay, and the person is discouraged not only about oppressive circumstances but also about his value as a human being. (Abnormal depression is often technically called "major depression" or "dysthmic disorder.") We are going to address abnormal depression in the next chapter, but at present we will look at normal depression.

## The Myth of the James Bond Christian

We may imagine that if we are mature psychologically and spiritually, we should be able to go through anything, any amount of suffering, loss, or affliction, and yet feel joyful through it all and victoriously bounce back.

But not so. I call this "the myth of the James Bond Christian." It is the misconception that normal humans can or should be like the movie superhero, James Bond, who tangles with supervillians as a way of life and never experiences painful emotions. He is as strong (and as cold) as steel. Should Christians really be like that fantasy hero?

A woman joined a friend's business and researched how to improve the operation. She backed up several suggestions with sound information on why her ideas would work and should be tried, but no one listened or gave her any recognition for her ideas. She was frustrated and discouraged at every turn. Soon she thought, "If I were a normal person, this would not be bothering me."

I told her I thought she had come by her depression honestly. It was a normal feeling. Of course, she felt discouraged. We are not James Bonds.

## The Depression of Paul

Did you know that the great Apostle Paul experienced depression? He is also the one who said, "I exhort you, therefore, be imitators of me" (1 Corinthians 4:16). Yet, Paul was one of the chief Christians of the Church Age and the single author contributing the most to the New Testament writings.

Sometimes we note his victorious moments and overlook his depressing ones. We like to think of the way Paul coped with his suffering in Philippi when he and Silas were in jail and sang hymns all night. What a way to go through trials — singing hymns all night! And while in jail!

However, Paul was quick to clarify that he did not always feel triumphant in trials. He included himself among those who have experienced depression: "God, who comforts the depressed, comforted us" (2 Corinthians 7:6), and "For we do not want you to be unaware, brethren, of our affliction which came to us in Asia, that we were burdened excessively, beyond our strength, so that we despaired even of life" (2 Corinthians 1:8). Sometimes he thought his sufferings were more than he could bear, and he even thought he would die of them. That is deep discouragement and depression.

At the same time, Paul also said he learned much that gave meaning and value to his depression and suffering. He explained that he learned to comfort others from the way God had comforted him:

> Blessed be the God and Father of our Lord Jesus Christ, the Father of mercies and God of all comfort; who comforts us in all our affliction so that we may be able to comfort those who are in any affliction with the comfort with which we ourselves are comforted by God. (2 Corinthians 1:3-4)

Because of his experiences, he is able to comfort us with these cherished words: "And we know that God causes all things to work together for good to those who love God, to those who are called according to His purpose" (Romans 8:28).

In case the example of Paul is not convincing enough to show that normal depression is not sinful or unspiritual, let's look at the example of our Lord and Savior Jesus Christ.

## The Depression of Jesus

Did you know that Jesus also experienced depression? In the Garden of Gethsemane, remember the agony and the depressed feelings he expressed?[1] Matthew 26:36-39 tells us,

> *Then Jesus came with them to a place called Gethsemane, and said to His disciples, "Sit here while I go over there and pray."*
>
> *And He took with Him Peter and the two sons of Zebedee, and began to be grieved and distressed.*
>
> *Then He said to them, "My soul is deeply grieved, to the point of death; remain here and keep watch with Me."*
>
> *And He went a little beyond them, and fell on His face and prayed, saying "My Father, if it is possible, let this cup pass from Me; yet not as I will, but as Thou wilt."*

That is depression!

In his grief and depression, he still had confidence in his Father's will, plan, and control. Even so, the circumstances had an emotional impact on him.

Luke 22:44 tells us that his depression was also accompanied by physical symptoms: "And being in agony He was praying very fervently; and His sweat became like drops of blood, falling down upon the ground." Can you see him kneeling—agony in his eyes, muscles strained from tension, perspiration flowing in rivulets from him?

This was the same Jesus who had said to his disciples only hours earlier, "These things I have spoken to you, that My joy may be in you, and that your joy may be made full" (John 15:11), and, "Peace I leave with you; My peace I give unto you" (John 14:27). We may well ask, "How do the depression and agony of Jesus go together with his joy and peace?"

Is it surprising that they are compatible? Sometimes the Gethsemane experience exemplifies what the peace and the joy of Jesus are like. Jesus' prayer in the Garden allows us to see into his thoughts and witness that in his most miserable hour, he trusted that his Father was in control and that the

132

present suffering was working out to a greater good. This faith was the source of Jesus' peace, confidence, and assurance of joy that accompanied his depression and distress.

Normal depression does not contradict the peace and joy of Jesus, especially when we go through it with the same confidence that Jesus had that the Father's will ultimately results in good.

Jesus was certainly spiritually mature, psychologically healthy, and morally perfect. Still he experienced depression. He was not James Bond either.

Both Jesus and Paul understood how to comfort and help us with depression and suffering, because they had been through it themselves. Moreover, their examples show that feeling depressed in painful circumstances is normal and not sinful or unspiritual.

## Avoiding Depression

Not everyone experiences depression. Some people seldom, if ever, allow themselves to feel normal emotional pain to any significant degree. Instead of putting themselves down, they inflate their self-image. They may blame everyone but themselves for their problems and may make others feel miserable. Or they may democratically minimize or explain away whatever is negative or painful in themselves, other people, and situations. Then, too, they may avoid pain by being on the move constantly—never sitting still or letting their minds rest, always stirring up excitement and activity.

Such personality styles may sound attractive in their own way. Wouldn't it be nice never to feel painful emotions?

The trouble is, however, that it is very difficult to run away from feelings and to resolve or learn from them at the same time. The only way never to suffer is to shut out emotions and never face them. This avoidance stunts growth. The Christian is called to "let endurance have its perfect result" in suffering (James 1:4) and to learn from the experiences of normal depression how to comfort others.

When people who have never experienced depression find

themselves experiencing it for the first time, it is often because one of life's experiences was finally so overwhelming that their usual methods of pain avoidance did not work. This pain can then motivate them to begin changing problems they have never before faced. Unfortunately, as the avoidance techniques start to succeed again, the immediate pain passes, and motivation to continue changing may evaporate. Such individuals will do well to decide, while they are still experiencing the pain, to finish the process of change — even if they feel better before the problems have been tackled.

## Cursing Fate

Those of us who experience normal depression may be tempted to react to suffering by cursing our fate. Unable to imagine any redeeming value to pain, we may cry out, "Why should this happen to me?"

One of my clients who struggles this way diagnoses himself as suffering from what he calls "the Little Caesar Complex." He means that he expects the world to treat him like an emperor and to cater to how he would like things to go.

For example, when he drives, he wishes to be king of the road. Streetlights should be timed to be always green, never red, for him. Other drivers should anticipate his every need and orchestrate themselves around him — never going too fast or too slow, always leaving him plenty of room to change lanes just when he wishes, and, of course, never cutting in front of him. Naturally, if pedestrians must cross in front of him, they should hurry and not hold him up too long. When any of this does not happen, he becomes resentful and even vengeful.

When life does not cooperate with our desires and we protest, "Why should this happen to me!" perhaps we ought to consider this also: "Why *shouldn't* it happen to me? Why should life spare me from living in the same fallen world with the same sinful people and unpleasant circumstances as everyone else has to live in?"

134

God originally designed perfect humans in a perfect world. Our sin changed all that. We are messed-up people, living in a broken world. (Genesis 3:17-19 uses the term *cursed*). Now God is using these imperfect, painful conditions to salvage at least some people who will become perfected by his mercy and power.

Suffering is inevitable for fallen people in a fallen world. God never promised us heaven on earth. In fact, we are quite frankly told we will suffer. This was made plain at the time of the Fall of man (Genesis 3), and Jesus' parting words at the end of his ministry reaffirmed the inevitability of suffering. But Jesus also gives us hope. "These things I have spoken to you," Jesus said, "that in Me you may have peace. In the world you have tribulation, but take courage; I have overcome the world" (John 16:33).

While the Old Testament promised present blessing as the reward for the righteous and present suffering as the punishment for the wicked, the New Testament (and part of the Old Testament, also) makes it clear that in this earthly life, the righteous will suffer and sometimes the wicked will prosper. Final reward and punishment are reserved for eternity. We might be tempted to believe that God hands us a guarantee that if we are good, everything will turn out rosy. Then when things do not work out that way, even though we are good, we may suppose God has cheated us. Bitterness toward him could be the likely next step.

Suffering can break us or make us, depending on whether we respond to it with bitterness or faith.

In times of pain, we may be tempted to become bitter toward God or others or to seek revenge. I remember kneeling and praying through my tears one time, shoving the couch into the wall with every syllable and saying, "Are you listening, God? Don't you care?" Honest anger with the openness to understand and to learn is, I believe, one normal reaction to suffering. In the process, wrestling with God and fighting bitterness may be necessary.

However, giving oneself over to bitterness and revenge is

self-destructive. Feeding and justifying bitterness is how Satan devours us in trials and temptations. Many a battle with temptation has been lost at the point where someone decided he or she had a right to surrender to bitterness.

Bitterness and revenge are to our souls what cancer is to our bodies.[2] They will consume and destroy us in a most miserable fashion. In chapter 3, I told how I overcame bitterness and forgave my enemies in a particular situation. It is imperative that we not return evil for evil, but let God (or his agents, such as the government—Romans 13:1-4) take care of any injustice in his own fair, objective, and merciful way (Romans 12:14, 17-21). Bitterness toward God or others is not a healing response to life's failure to cooperate with our wishes.

## Purposes of Suffering

The Scriptures reveal that there are various purposes God intends suffering to serve in our lives

*Discipline.* One purpose of suffering is discipline. A college student raced down a country road in his beloved sports car, a Triumph. He was on his way to a "beer bust," where he knew he would give into immorality. "O God," he prayed, "help me. You know I am weak." Just then, his wheel caught on a telephone pole that had fallen by some freak accident and had rolled onto the road just enough to catch his wheel. The car turned and slammed into a tree. As he pulled his head out of the windshield, he felt overwhelmed by the presence of God's love. He felt God had loved him enough to discipline him and to save him from the weakest part of himself.

No longer having a means of transportation, he had to walk to his classes on campus the next day. In so doing, he passed a building where he overheard the singing of Christian songs. He discovered a Christian student fellowship and joined it. Now he considers the wreck of his Triumph a form of discipline that God used to give him victory and help him grow. Somewhat humorously, he likes to imagine that the Apostle Paul was referring to his car when Paul said, "But

thanks be to God, who always leads us in His triumph . . . "
(2 Corinthians 2:14).

One of the most revealing passages about God's discipline
is Hebrews 12:

> My son, do not regard lightly the discipline of the Lord, nor
> faint when you are reproved by Him; for those whom the Lord
> loves He disciplines, and He scourges every son whom He
> receives.
>
> It is for discipline that you endure; God deals with you as
> with sons; for what son is there whom his father does not dis-
> cipline? But if you are without discipline, of which all have be-
> come partakers, then you are illegitimate children and not
> sons.
>
> Furthermore, we had earthly fathers to discipline us, and
> we respected them; shall we not much rather be subject to the
> Father of spirits, and live?
>
> For they disciplined us for a short time as seemed best to
> them, but He disciplines us for our good, that we may share
> His holiness.
>
> All discipline for the moment seems not to be joyful, but sor-
> rowful; yet to those who have been trained by it, afterwards it
> yields the peaceful fruit of righteousness. (Hebrews 12:5b-11)

The college student accurately understood the nature of
God's discipline. God's motive is love, not anger. His objective is to teach, not to get even or to make us pay for our sins.
Remember, Jesus has satisfied God's anger at sin, having paid
for our sins already. If we have settled our worthiness of
God's acceptance by receiving Jesus' gift, we need fear no
punishment. Divine discipline has no penal aspect. Instead,
God's purpose is to develop our competence in the maturation of character and development of abilities.

*Personal Growth.* Some people think that every time they
suffer, it is because they did something wrong and God is disciplining them. Not so. There is another purpose for suffer-

ing—personal growth. To paraphrase E. Stanley Jones, a great missionary to Africa: "I don't bear sorrow, trouble, sickness, and death. I use them."[3]

The Apostle James, brother of our Lord Jesus, also said, "Consider it all joy, my brethren, when you encounter various trials; knowing that the testing of your faith produces endurance. And let endurance have its perfect result, that you may be perfect and complete, lacking in nothing" (James 1:2-4).

Several times I have undergone depressing crises for which, in retrospect, I have blessed God. One played an especially significant role in my personal development. The fall of my freshman year in college, I was engaged to marry a young man who broke our engagement just before Christmas. Some of the Christmas presents I received were actually wedding gifts. On Christmas Day, I was opening presents for a wedding that was not to be. That was the most miserable Christmas of my life.

For days afterward, I would sometimes momentarily be laughing and thinking about something entirely different from the broken engagement and then suddenly start to cry. I felt as though my life had been reduced to zero. I was extremely depressed.

At that time, my father gave me considerable support and shared Scripture on how he thought the Lord was going to be with me and strengthen me through this period. I began to consider, by faith, that there might be some positive outcome.

As I seriously thought about my relationship with the Lord, I began to gain insights that made the event a turning point in my life. Up until then, I had expected my life's fulfillment would be dependent on a husband who would inject self-esteem and security into my soul as I desperately clung to him for these things. I would have suffocated the poor guy. The breaking of the engagement made me realize that even if I had a man, he could be taken from me. My dependence had been misdirected.

I believe the Lord wanted me to find my primary and unchangeable security in him, along with becoming a full person in my own right. I began thanking the Lord for what I was undergoing even though I still felt miserable. I was even able to say, "I'd be willing to go through this a hundred times for what I am getting out of it."

As I look back, I also am thankful because the Lord enabled me to meet and marry my husband, Terry, the right person for me. By remaining single longer, I was able to spend more years in school, years that I found stimulating and enjoyable. I was also able to become a psychologist with a fulfilling career to which I believe the Lord has called me. What a gigantic lesson and fortunate turn of events at the price of losing a marriage that would have been premature for me anyway!

This broken engagement, along with other times of heartbreak and disappointment, has led me to one conclusion: *Some of my worst times have actually been my best times.*


*To the Glory of God.*   We do not always get to know the reason for our pain. Job never knew. Neither did his friends who erroneously assumed that he was being disciplined. The point of Job's trials was not primarily discipline or personal growth.

The Book of Job tells us what the purpose may be when it is not readily apparent in this life. We are explicitly told that Job suffered—not that he might be disciplined or matured, but that he might serve as an example of holiness to someone else. Job was God's "Exhibit A."

Job lost literally everything in one day. He lost his children, his possessions, and his health. He even had to endure the so-called comfort of friends who falsely accused him, thus kicking him while he was down and when he needed caring the most. Still, in spite of all his hardship, he never sinned or cursed God. In fact, Job said, "Naked I came from my mother's womb, and naked I shall return there. The Lord gave and the Lord has taken away. Blessed be the name of the Lord" (Job 1:21).

Job was put out of commission by his calamity and suffering. He could not even "serve" God in the active, overt sense. But he *was* serving God more than he ever dreamed – by *how* he suffered and by the kind of person he was *being*. His example has brought great glory to God. As a model for humankind, he has demonstrated how suffering itself can be turned into a form of worship. The suffering of Job exposed him for what he really was – a beautiful human being who radiated the glory of God.

When I think of a modern-day Job, a person whose suffering was primarily for the sake of others and for the glory of God, I think of Corrie ten Boom, the Dutch woman who in the middle of her hitherto uneventful life found herself suffering in World War II under the Nazi occupation. She became part of an underground movement to harbor Jews, aiding them in escaping for their lives. Eventually, Corrie herself was confined in a prison camp where she suffered many humiliations and much deprivation, not the least of which was the death of her sister.[4]

Who knew of or cared about her suffering? Many people: the Jews she helped save, fellow prisoners to whom she ministered the Word and love of God, and all of us who have heard of her example. There was another audience of onlookers who benefited from her suffering: her enemies.

One day, Corrie was telling her story and speaking at a church about forgiveness. After the service, a man came forward to speak to her. He confessed to having been one of the guards who had caused her suffering, and he asked her forgiveness.[5] Corrie herself had not known the impact she had had as God's "Exhibit A." That knowledge gave her great joy as she saw what God was able to accomplish through her suffering.

Jesus also suffered for the sake of others. Why? Hebrews reveals the reason – "for the joy set before Him" – the joy of the reward of reigning with the Father (12:2), but also the joy of rescuing us, of being able to have us as his brothers and sisters, and of being able to understand, through his firsthand experiences, our suffering so he can mercifully and faithfully help us (2:9-18). The greatest joy is the joy of loving. Jesus suffered for the deepest fulfillment that comes with giving for another's good.

In heaven, I suspect our greatest joy may not be when *God praises us* and says, "Well done, good and faithful slave [servant]; you were faithful with a few things, I will put you in charge of many things; enter into the joy of your master" (Matthew 25:21). Rather, I think our greatest joy will be when *we worship him* for his having worked through us and when we see others who are there because of what God has chosen to do through us.

## Support Network

God's ideal is for us to have a network of supportive Christians to help us during our depression and to help us to suffer successfully, that is, to have faith in God's purposes. The body of Christ should serve this purpose.

Sometimes it does, and sometimes it doesn't.

For example, what happens when a couple in a church has marital problems or separates? Typically, one or both parties do not dare to talk about it at church because of guilt or fear of judgmental attitudes. Another danger also exists—church members who try to comfort by taking sides, telling each person what he or she wants to hear even when it is not true or helpful, condemning without understanding both sides, or counseling the couple to give up hastily and put themselves out of their misery.

Subsequently, the separated or divorced person is, more than likely, in danger of social isolation. No one is sure what to say to him or to her, and it is hard to be patient enough to support the sufferers as long as may be necessary. Then, too, it may be awkward to invite a single person to a social occasion attended by couples. To the extent that the church is couple or family oriented, people with troubled marriages may feel out of place and sense the need to change churches or to drop out altogether to survive emotionally.

By contrast, I know of a church that provided emotional and spiritual support for a suffering couple. The couple had left another church because they realized it would be unwise for them to disclose their marital problems there. They found support at this other church that had numerous small groups, which met regularly. Each spouse went into a separate support group at first. Since the husband was tempted toward unfaithfulness and was still struggling with whether to commit himself to the marriage, he did not feel ready to join a couples' support group with his wife.

For months, their new Christian friends bathed each one with support. They visited, called, loved, and prayed with them individually. Their prayers were fervent with faith and called on God's power to help both spouses.

In the small group meetings, people were open about their problems and were amazed to discover how serious the problems of their fellow "average" Christian friends were. Discovering they were not unique or weird in their struggles provided a measure of healing: It was a relief not to have to carry the heavy load of secrets behind a smiling facade! It was wonderful to experience strong, warm love and the ever available power of God the Holy Spirit!

In time, the husband felt ready to visit his wife's support group. The group members welcomed him lovingly and nonjudgmentally. They were open to understanding his feelings, too. Finally, he felt ready to work on the marriage to see if it could be different than it had been before. The couple went for marriage counseling with a professional Christian counselor and continued in their support group. Sometimes the group confronted one or both of them, but these confrontations were loving and supportive. Unfortunately, the husband listened to the wrong advice from other people who encouraged him to divorce his wife and leave the church support group.

Naturally, the wife felt devastated by her husband's behavior. What helped bring her through her grief was the warmth and encouragement of her support group. In time, she experienced not only that life has a way of going on, but that God also has new plans in store for his children. She eventually found meaning to her suffering when she was able to use the lessons she had learned to help others.

The small group grew in confidence and faith. They were experiencing what James described: "Therefore, confess your sins to one another, and pray for one another, so that you may be healed. The effective prayer of a righteous man can accomplish much." (James 5:16)

If you don't have this kind of support from a small group or from at least one close friend, you need to have it, whether or not you are currently struggling. You cannot get through life without facing pain. When it comes, true Christian fellowship will help you not just go through it, but *grow* through it.

### The Right Response to Normal Depression

How should we respond to normal pain or the depression that accompanies suffering?

James says, "Consider it all joy . . ." (James 1:2a) and "confess your sins to one another, and pray for one another, so that you may be healed . . ." (5:16).

Paul says, "Rejoice always; pray without ceasing; in everything give thanks; for this is God's will for you in Christ Jesus. Do not quench the Holy Spirit; . . . abstain from every form of evil" (1 Thessalonians 5:16-19, 22).

Rejoicing in trials and confessing our faults are not always easy. Thanking God for them is often an expression of faith more than of emotion. At the same time, Scripture is realistic in stating that suffering "for the moment seems not to be joyful, but sorrowful" (Hebrews 12:11). Even Jesus, David, and Paul experienced deep depression. It is, after all, "the depressed" (2 Corinthians 7:6) that God comforts.

143

## Summing It Up

Normal depression is not harmful or destructive. We need not avoid or resent it. If responded to in faith, it can work as discipline or instruction to perfect us as the images of God, making us competent in character and skills for reigning with Christ. "If we endure, we shall also reign with Him" (2 Timothy 2:12).

Think of the times you have personally grown the most. Weren't the majority of them times of suffering? Christian fellowship is valuable to help us in our time of need. And our going through difficult times with faith may benefit others and glorify God.

If you are laying guilt on yourself for feeling normal depression, get off your own back. Start walking the road to wholeness!

## Target Questions

1. Does the title of this chapter "Is My Depression Normal?" surprise you? Have you ever thought depression could be normal? Why or why not?

2. The chapter opens with many examples of depressing circumstances. When you encounter depressing experiences, what tends to be your usual response? Is it any of the following?

    A. I try not to feel badly or think about it. Why hurt? It doesn't do any good. Better to keep busy, cheer myself up, and forget about it. If you don't think about problems, maybe they will go away.

    B. I feel depressed and then kick myself for being "unspiritual," "abnormal," or "immature." I think I should be a "James Bond Christian."

    C. I replay my critical tapes. I tell myself the negative

events prove I don't belong, am worthless, or am incompetent.

D. I automatically believe God is disciplining me, even if I know of nothing I've done wrong.

E. I get angry at God and/or others, cursing my fate and wondering why "this" had to happen to me. The "Little Caesar" attitude describes my response.

F. I try to allow myself to experience all my feelings, whatever they are. When I'm confused, I ask God to help me pinpoint what I am feeling. There's no emotion too awful to admit, and no harm will come from experiencing what emotion is there.

I use feelings, even painful ones, as information or cues to show me when a problem still exists and needs my attention. Then I open up my feelings to God for his understanding and help.

When I need to, I reach out for the support of loved ones, too. I try to thank God, by faith, for negative events, especially the worst points, so that I can begin to imagine what could possibly be good about them (Romans 8:28). Seeing meaning or purpose in my suffering sustains me as I go through it. Then my responses are more constructive and loving, and I feel myself maturing, deepening, broadening more into the person I'd love to be. That feels good!

3. Imagine that a loved one has died and you are at the funeral. Which of the following attitudes seems most wholesome for you to adopt? Why?

A. Why be sad! He's (She's) in heaven now! The funeral is merely a celebration!

B. My loved one is in heaven now, and that is wonderful for him (her), but I will miss him (her) so much! I need this funeral to help me express my grief and say farewell, so I can face my loss and find a place in me to put my memories. The funeral will serve little purpose for my loved one. It is for me and others who mourn and for those who came to show loving support for us who mourn.

4. Many Bible characters suffered normal depression as the examples below illustrate:

Nehemiah (Nehemiah 2:1-4)
Esther (Esther 4)
Hannah (1 Samuel 1)
David (Psalm 32)
Jesus, Lazarus, Mary, Martha (John 11:4-5, 14-15, 32-45)
Philippian jailor (Acts 16:23-34)
Paul (Philippians 4:11-13)

Which of the following do you think was the primary purpose for the suffering of each of these particular characters in the passages given above?

    A. Discipline

    B. Personal growth or benefit

    C. Benefit of others and glory of God

5. Can you think of a time that you suffered and the purpose was one of those suggested in question 4?

6. When you hurt, whom can you talk to? Who listens, cares, and prays for you? Do you do the same for someone? Who? If you don't have this kind of relationship with anyone, ask yourself this question: "Who would I like for my friend if I could have whoever I wanted? Is this someone God would approve of my having for a friend?" (If not, keep thinking of people you'd like for friends till you think of someone God would agree is good for you.) Then consider these ques-

tions: "How can I befriend this person? How can I initiate contact in an appropriate way?"

Are you a member of a Christian support group, such as a Bible study or fellowship group where people share their concerns, listen to each other, and pray for one another? If not, do you know anyone who might like to form one with you?

7. If you are suffering right now through something big or small, tell God how you *honestly* feel about it, whether you think your feelings are right or not. Then thank God by faith for allowing this negative circumstance to come into your life and ask him to help you see some positive purposes in it.

If you wish, share your feelings and prayer request with someone else. Pray together.

If you are studying this book with a group, take time for group members to share their concerns and pray for one another.

# 9
# WHEN IS MY DEPRESSION ABNORMAL?

Can you guess who wrote these words?

> I am forty-five years old. Two-thirds of a long life have
> passed, and I have done nothing to distinguish it by
> usefulness to my country and to mankind. . . . Pas-
> sions, indolence, weakness and infirmities have some-
> times made me swerve from my better knowledge of
> right and almost constantly paralyzed my efforts of
> good.[1]

At age seventy, this same person wrote that his "whole life
has been a succession of disappointments. I can scarcely
recollect a single instance of success in anything that I ever
undertook."[2]

The author of these self-evaluations was John Quincy
Adams, sixth president of the United States and a man of
strong Puritan faith. President John F. Kennedy was later to
say of him,

> John Quincy Adams – until his death at eighty in the
> Capitol – held more important offices and partici-
> pated in more important events than anyone in the
> history of our nation, as Minister to The Hague, Emis-
> sary to England, Minister to England, Secretary of
> State, President of the United States, and member of
> the House of Representatives. He figured in one capac-
> ity or another, in the American Revolution, The War

of 1812 and the prelude to the Civil War. Among the acquaintances and colleagues who march across the pages of his diary are Sam Adams (a kinsman), John Hancock, Washington, Jefferson, Franklin, Lafayette, John Jay, James Madison, James Monroe, John Marshall, Henry Clay, Andrew Jackson, Thomas Hart Benton, John Tyler, John C. Calhoun, Daniel Webster, Lincoln, James Buchanan, William Lloyd Garrison, Andrew Johnson, Jefferson Davis and many others.[3]

Kennedy eulogized Quincy as "one of the most talented men ever to serve his nation,"[4] whose life "has never been paralleled in American history."[5]

How could a man of such stature and outstanding accomplishment see himself as a failure?

## What Is Abnormal Depression?

For Adams, as for any abnormally depressed person, an experience of loss, threatened loss, setback or failure, discouragement, or disillusionment opened the floodgate for an onslaught of his critical tapes. What distinguishes abnormal depression from normal depression is the presence of critical tapes.

When an abnormally depressed person suffers, he or she begins replaying critical tapes, because the adverse circumstances are taken as proof that the critical tapes are true. The oppression of the critical tapes then causes psychological and physical symptoms.

For an abnormally depressed person:

1. Life loses its flavor.
2. Former pleasures from work, family, or friends may be lost.
3. Interests narrow.
4. Efficiency is generally reduced.
5. The individual may complain of being unable to concentrate, to remember, to understand what is said, or to

think clearly. That is, what initially appears as a problem of feelings also shows itself to be a problem in the way a person is *thinking*.

6. Enjoyment of adult responsibilities slips away. In fact, the sufferer may want to withdraw. Normal activity may feel like an unbearable load.

These psychological symptoms are frequently accompanied by physical symptoms. While the most common physical symptoms are sleep disturbance, change in appetite, and loss of sexual interest, there may be others as well.

Dr. Nathan Kline, a psychiatrist who has been a leading researcher on depression and who discovered the first anti-depressant medication in 1953,[6] includes the following symptoms as typical of abnormal depression. He indicates that an abnormally depressed person experiences some combination from among the following possible symptoms in degrees that may vary from mild to severe.[7]

- Reduced enjoyment and pleasure (even if the feeling of depression is not present), boredom, rejection of opportunities, general loss of interest
- Poor concentration, slowed thinking, poor memory
- Fatigue
- Remorse
- Guilt (about decreased ability to function and the consequent impact on others)
- Indecision
- Financial concern (fear of using up resources, sometimes with marked underestimation of what one can afford)
- Decreased love and affection, social withdrawal
- Reduced sexual activity
- Tearfulness
- Gloominess about the future
- Irritability
- Suicidal thoughts (Almost everyone thinks of suicide at one time or another, but such thoughts are more frequent during abnormal depression.)

- Unusual thoughts or urges (for example, fear that a loved one will die, or urge to harm a loved one)
- Evasive, vague, ponderous communication (when not typical for the person)
- Emotionally flat responses
- Decreased tidiness in dress and appearance
- Slack posture and hesitant, uncertain walking
- Increased clumsiness
- Fear that one is dying (and the doctors won't tell the "truth" about it)
- Focus on aches and pains (real or imagined)
- Constipation
- Dry mouth
- Sleep disturbance (with insomnia and early morning awakening most common)
- Loss of appetite with possible weight loss; otherwise, overeating

---

**Physical Symptoms of Anxiety That May Accompany Depression**

Nausea

Chest pains

Stomach cramps

Rapid breathing

Sweating

Coldness of extremities (hands, feet)

Numbness

Tingling of the hands and feet

Headaches or other odd feelings of pressure in the head, ears, or neck

---

From my personal observations, I have noted that many Christians who became abnormally depressed discover they feel as distant from God as they do from people they usually love. It may be difficult for them to feel the presence of God, to believe he hears their prayers, or to hope he will actually help them. Not realizing that this pessimism and numbing of emotions is merely a symptom of abnormal depression, they may conclude that God has rejected them or that they have lost their salvation. Or, due to their critical tapes replaying, abnormally depressed persons may exaggerate their sins and feel certain God could never forgive them.

Abnormal depression clearly has a far-reaching impact on those afflicted with it. It is also, unfortunately, a widespread emotional problem.

---

**Statistics on Abnormal Depression**

As many as 15 percent of all adults between 18 and 74 may suffer from abnormal depression in a given year. If left alone to run its natural course, it lasts about 6 months to a year on the *average* — sometimes much longer.[8]

---

Critical tapes certainly take their toll!

## Dysfunctional Thinking

Let's look at the role critical tapes play in bringing about abnormal depression with all its painful symptoms.

A person who is prone to abnormal depression may not hear critical tapes all the time, especially when other things are going well. However, in times of stress, the critical tapes replay so convincingly as to seem overwhelming. The abnormally depressed person often supposes that anyone in the same circumstances would feel the same way. The critical tapes appear to be a true description of reality to the sufferer, even though they appear farfetched to other people and also to the sufferer when he or she is not abnormally depressed.

Unpleasant — even extremely traumatic — life situations do not necessarily lead to abnormal depression unless the person has particularly ingrained critical tapes specifically related to the type of situation that is causing suffering. In response to extremely adverse circumstances, the average person will still maintain interest in and realistically interpret other nontraumatic aspects of his or her life. The thinking of the abnormally depressed person, by contrast, becomes obsessed with, and colored by, critical tapes.

The abnormally depressed person is one whose thoughts are dominated by critical tapes to the point that this person *distorts reality* to fit the critical tapes. It seldom occurs to the abnormally depressed person, however, that his or her way of thinking is illogical or unrealistic. The critical tapes are accepted unquestioningly.

Dr. Aaron Beck, a leading researcher in the psychotherapeutic treatment of depression, has written much on the reasoning processes of the abnormally depressed.[9] I will adapt his perspective on this.

The following are examples of how the abnormally depressed person replaces realistic and logical thinking with dysfunctional thinking based on critical tapes. The abnormally depressed person in our illustration is a sixth-grade teacher who suffers from a critical tape that says, "I am incompetent." She has just received from her principal an evaluation that rates her skills above average overall but unsatisfactory in communicating math concepts. Examples of her dysfunctional thinking are contrasted with illustrations of rational and realistic thinking.[10] You will see how she distorts logic and reality to make them support her critical tape.

## Dysfunctional Thinking

## Rational and Realistic Thinking

1. NONDIMENSIONAL AND GLOBAL:
   "I am completely incompetent."

1. MULTIDIMENSIONAL:
   "I am good at teaching most subjects, but I have difficulty making math clear to my sixth graders."

2. ABSOLUTISTIC AND MORALISTIC:
   "I am a no-good failure."

2. RELATIVISTIC AND NONJUDGMENTAL:
   "I have more difficulty teaching math than most teachers I know."

3. INVARIANT:
   "I always have been and always will be incapable. I'm hopeless."

3. VARIABLE:
   "I teach some subjects better than others."

4. CHARACTER DIAGNOSIS:
   "I have a defect in my character."

4. BEHAVIORAL DIAGNOSIS:
   "I am afraid I can't teach math well, and I procrastinate in preparing my lessons."

5. IRRVERSIBILITY:
   "Since I am basically inept, there is nothing that can be done about it. I am hopeless."

5. REVERSIBILITY:
   "I can learn ways of starting lessons plans earlier and can take workshops to improve my skills for teaching math."

6. SELECTIVE OBSERVATION:
   "The principal rated me low on communicating math concepts."

6. OBSERVING THE WHOLE:
   "The principal rated me above average on all other job skills and commented that we have a very poor textbook for math this year."

7. MAGNIFICATION:
   "One parent complained that I wasn't helping his son learn math well enough. This must be how all the parents feel about me."

7. REALISTIC EVALUATION OF SIGNIFICANCE OF A SITUATION:
   "One parent disliked one thing."

8. MINIMIZATION:
   "The principal complimented my teaching today. She was just being nice."

8. REALISTIC EVALUATION OF SIGNIFICANCE OF A SITUATION:
   "The principal thinks I am doing well overall."

155

| Dyfunctional Thinking | Rational and Realistic Thinking |
|---|---|
| 9. PERSONALIZATION: "A group of parents after a PTA meeting are across the room talking to each other. They are probably criticizing the way I teach." | 9. REALISTIC ASSESSMENT OF WHETHER EXTERNAL EVENTS RELATE TO ONESELF: "There is a group discussion going on. It is highly unlikely that their thoughts revolve around me." |
| 10. ALL-OR-NOTHING DICHOTOMOUS THINKING: "Either I am totally competent or I am totally incompetent. Since I believe I am not totally competent, I must therefore be totally incompetent." | 10. MULTIDIMENSIONAL AND RELATIVISTIC THINKING: "Some of my teaching skills are better than others. Some days I teach better than others. God loves me through it all." |
| 11. CATASTROPHIC THINKING: "Since the principal rated me low on communicating math skills, I will lose my job, and that will mean I'll lose my house and car, and that will mean my husband will divorce me, and that will mean I will never see my kids again, and then my whole life will be ruined." | 11. ACCURATE PREDICTION OF FUTURE: "The principal rated me above average overall. I will still have my job, and very little if anything in my life will be affected. I will take effective steps to improve in teaching math, and then I will have even less to be anxious about. Besides, God is still in control and will help me in any event." |

As you read the examples of her irrationally and unrealistically negativistic thinking, could you sense how they would weigh a person down with hopelessness, low self-esteem, and depression?

And as you read the rational and realistic alternatives, did you feel as though a refreshing mind-set of peace and optimism was restored?

No wonder the Apostle Paul prescribed the following antidote to abnormal depression:

> *Finally, brethren, whatever is true, whatever is honorable, whatever is right, whatever is pure, whatever is lovely, whatever is of good repute, if there is any excellence and if anything worthy of praise, let your mind dwell on these things.* (Philippians 4:8)

*Testing Dysfunctional Thoughts.* When we are depressed, how can we test the validity of our thinking to find out whether it is the *dysfunctional type* or the *rational and realistic type* illustrated here?

1. Check whether our thoughts seem to resemble the examples of dysfunctional thinking or rational and realistic thinking described in the above illustration.

For instance, I recall many times as a teenager getting what I considered a low grade. I would walk the whole mile home absorbed in catastrophic thinking:

"My low grade on this assignment means I will surely get a low grade for the course, and then I will have a low grade point average, and then I won't be able to get into as good a college, and then I won't get to meet the kind of men I'd like to marry; and then my whole life will be ruined!"

Had I been exposed to examples of catastrophic thinking, I might have realized what an enormous jump I was making from a poor grade on one assignment to the ruination of my entire life.

2. Try to imagine that someone else is going through our troubles and expressing the same thoughts.

Does it seem realistic, for example, for the other person to conclude that he or she is "completely incompetent," "a no-good failure," "hopeless," and so on? Sometimes role playing will help us picture talking to someone who is in our shoes. Most of us when abnormally depressed can be more objective for someone else than for ourselves.

3. Test whether there is any past evidence to disconfirm our conclusions.

For instance, the sufferer might ask, "Am I really *completely* incompetent? Was there *ever* a time I felt more competent than I do now? Was there *ever* a time I did something well? Have I *ever* gotten positive feedback from anyone about my competence?"

4. Think of any possible alternative explanations for our personalized and negativistic interpretations of the behavior of others.

The discouraged teacher in our illustration needed to think of any other possible explanation for what a group of parents across the room could possibly be discussing besides her teaching ability.

5. Run experiments to collect adequate data that will allow us to confirm or disconfirm our depressing beliefs or hypotheses.

In our illustration, the teacher could test her hypothesis of total incompetence. She might test her competence for each lesson (not only math lessons) as she presents it during the course of the day, and repeat this procedure for a week. She could do this by predicting ahead of time what she believes her competence level will be. (She could use a rating from 1 to 100, 1 being totally incompetent, 50 being medium competence, and 100 being perfection itself.) Then she could re-rate her competence after giving each lesson to test her beliefs (ratings) about her competence.

Comparing her predictions to her evaluations of her actual competence could go a long way to effectively correct her negativistic thinking against reality. If it does not, she is probably so deeply immersed in her distorted thinking that she would do well to seek professional help to correct it.

6. Test the validity of our thinking against the revealed truth of Scripture.

For instance, do the Scriptures support the belief that "I am completely incompetent?" No. First Corinthians 12 says the Holy Spirit has gifted me with certain spiritual abilities that benefit others.

Does "failure" make me "no good" or "unlovable"? No, because the Apostle Paul tells us in Romans 8:38-39:

> For I am convinced that neither death, nor life, nor angels, nor principalities, nor things present, nor things to come, nor powers, nor height, nor depth, nor any other created thing, shall be able to separate us from the love of God, which is in Christ Jesus our Lord.

I listed the test of Scripture last. Why? Because many abnormally depressed people, due to their dysfunctional thinking, minimize the applicability of scriptural reassurances for themselves or, after deriving temporary comfort, cannot hang onto them for long. They may think biblical insights are wonderful for others, but see themselves as exceptions.

In addition, any criticism of their lack of faith (or of anything else) is only likely to reinforce the self-criticism from which they already suffer. They often first have to be helped to use specific logical and experimental tests, such as those described above, to correct the dysfunctional thinking caused by their critical tapes. Then they become more able to hear the Scriptures accurately and apply them personally.

## Depression and Selflessness

While abnormal depression usually refers to an unrealistically and irrationally low view of one's value due to critical tape thinking, depression can be a secondary symptom accompanying other emotional problems.

As a chief example, some people have a low view of themselves because they have little sense of being a self at all. Their critical tapes have resulted in more than low self-esteem. They do not really ever exercise their selfhood. They feel that, to be secure and able to fulfill normal adult responsibilities, they must cling dependently to another person who, they hope, will enable them to function. If that person either does not take care of them as hoped or leaves the relationship, they feel abandoned and lost. Depression, anger, fear, guilt, passivity and helplessness, and emptiness and void—emotions that these individuals are forever fighting against—come to the fore.

*Early Childhood.* How does an individual come to lack a sense of selfhood? During the first few years of life, particularly ages fifteen months to twenty-two months, a child normally is developing awareness of being an individual self. During this critical phase, some children may have experienced inadequate emotional support, because the mother felt anxious about her child growing up. When the child attempted to develop normal skills that would lead to increased independence, the mother became emotionally distant or attacking.

One such mother, for example, saw her baby beginning to walk and thought, *Now she doesn't need me.* This mother became less involved, to the point that she did not protect her exploring toddler from impending accidents.

Another mother, experiencing for the first time that her

two year old was discovering she could make choices and say no, verbally attacked her little daughter, shouting threateningly, "Don't you ever say 'no' to me again!" She never did. Nor did she say "no" to anyone else either.

As a young adult, she was unassertive and did not protect herself or make the decisions necessary to handle the adult responsibilities of independent living. She went to bed with any man who asked, because she was afraid to say no. By her severe passivity, she was also expressing her anger about not having the right to have a will and be the person of her own choosing. She had obeyed her mother to the extreme, as if to say "OK, I will *never* say no, and you'll be sorry!" Now she was also allowing herself to be treated as the worthless thing she felt she was.

Sometimes, parental support is not available during the first few years for other reasons, such as hospitalization of the mother or of the infant that keeps them apart, prolonged travel by the parents without the baby, marital separations, death of a parent, birth of a sickly brother or sister who absorbs all the mother's attention, or inadequate provision for child care while parents are working.

If, in addition, the child subsequently is traumatized by such things as sexual molestation, physical abuse that is experienced or observed, or alcoholism[11] in the home, and learns to cope with such terrifying events by denying and not expressing his or her true thoughts and feelings about what happened, the pattern of not exercising the inner self can become entrenched.

*Lifelong Conflicts.* Children who do not receive adequate, loving support for becoming their unique selves and for utilizing their God-created capacities to employ good judgment, to think, to feel, and to make choices for themselves are likely to wind up stumbling through life as "nonpersons." There may be chronic chaos in their most intimate relationships, their sexual activities, their parenting of their own children, and their school and job performance.

161

Whenever they need to activate the inner self to take charge of a normal responsibility, they tend to become depressed, to fail to even try, and to engage in some activity to numb the depression — activities such as alcohol or drug abuse, literally running away, sexual promiscuity, spending too much money, binge eating, dangerous thrill-seeking, cutting school or not showing up at work, or developing emotional dependency on their children or on someone else. They may both crave and fear wholesome intimacy.

Professional counseling is often advisable to enable them to experience insight into their self-destructive behavior and to help them begin to exercise the inner self. Frequently, Christian counseling is even essential.

If such an individual has, unfortunately, been taught that the self is the same as the old sin nature, that therefore to exercise our God-created capacities is to live "in the flesh," or that Christians should be "selfless," it may be even more confusing for this person to sort out how to activate the inner self and be a Christian, too. Experiencing that self-activation and Christian maturity are complementary, not contradictory, may take time. A Christian professional counselor experienced in treating people with an inadequate sense of self can be of immeasurable help.

## When to Get Professional Treatment

When self-help material of the sort provided here and other means of assistance such as the support of loved ones or pastoral counseling are not sufficient to relieve abnormal depression, professional help should be seriously considered for several reasons:

1. In about half of all abnormal depressions, there is evidence of physical illness.

Physical illness is rated by some as the *fifth* most common type of incident precipitating the beginning of abnormal depression. Therefore, sufferers, especially where there was no apparent nonmedical problem, event, or emotional stress that brought on the abnormal depression, should get a physical checkup.

---

**Facts about the Physical Side of Depression**

1. Some physical disorders associated with abnormal depression are:

   - Thyroid, adrenal, and parathyroid dysfunctions
   - pernicious anemia
   - viral infections
   - cancer
   - epilepsy
   - vitamin deficiencies
   - rheumatoid arthritis. [12]

2. Drugs that can cause the "depressive syndrome" are:

   - reserpine
   - alphamethyldopa (an antihypertensive)
   - propranolol (cardiac drug)
   - birth-control pills
   - steroids. [13]

3. A physical cause of depression in 40 percent of women of menstruating age is premenstrual syndrome, which is now medically treatable. [14]

4. Sometimes both physical illiness and psychological stress precede the onset of abnormal depression.

---

It has been found that as many as 18 percent of abnormally depressed persons may be suffering from a lithium deficiency. [15] If deficient, lithium, a biochemical salt normally present in our bodies, can cause a person to undergo endless mood cycles, becoming alternately depressed or manic.

*Manic* refers to the euphoric mood opposite of abnormal depression and is usually accompanied by an extremely inflated ego, irrationally and unrealistically positive thinking, high energy, and excessive pursuit of exciting and stimulating experiences (e.g., through immoral behavior or particularly uninhibited forms of fun and entertainment). A person who has a lithium deficiency is diagnosed as "manicdepressive," or as having a "bipolar mood disorder." The only known effective treatment is medication (namely lithium in most cases).

2. The relief of the human misery experienced by the sufferer and his or her frustrated family is another reason to get professional help.

The best way to prevent future recurrences of depression is by helping the sufferer to function fully at work and in relationships and to overcome the replay of critical tapes and irrationally and unrealistically negative thinking habits. The appropriate kinds of professionals to see to accomplish these types of changes are mental health professionals.

3. Because of the potential for suicide in severe abnormal depression, professional psychotherapy is advisable.

If a depressed person expresses suicidal wishes, the danger of suicide should be taken seriously and professional help should be sought immediately. Most people who attempt suicide and are rescued by professional treatment discover within a few days that they are glad to be alive.[16] This was true of Linda whose story began this book. However, because of their dysfunctional thinking, suicidally depressed individuals are often unable to predict they will ever feel better.

**Medication – Pro and Con**
Before ending this discussion on abnormal depression, I would like to add a word about antidepressant medication

(as prescribed by a physician, preferably a psychiatrist). In a number of cases of abnormal depression, a physiological change (namely catecholamine deficiency) is known to occur in the brain chemistry of the sufferer. When this medical problem is corrected by an antidepressant (of the type and at the dosage appropriate for the individual), the habitual irrational and unrealistic negative thinking drastically decreases, usually around three to four weeks after beginning medication.

This medication must be taken for the period of time prescribed by a physician. It is estimated that as many as 55 percent of persons treated with antidepressants will have no subsequent episodes of depression. However, according to one study, 36 percent who receive no psychotherapy after discontinuing medication relapsed into abnormal depression within eight months.[17] Some studies have shown that treating the dysfunctional thinking, when systematically done by a trained professional, can be at least as effective as antidepressant medication for some individuals,[18] while a combination of medication and psychotherapy is most effective for many sufferers. Some sufferers need antidepressant medication in order to be able to benefit from counseling.

Antidepressant medication is not a cure-all for everyone who suffers from abnormal depression, but it is medically needed by many such individuals. It is *absolutely not addicting*, and for those who need it, it is *not a "crutch."* I personally have treated many abnormally depressed persons who, in the opinion of myself and the physician involved in the case, definitely needed antidepressant medication, but who felt their spirituality or strength of character was being judged by well-meaning Christian family members and friends. The abnormally depressed person often is already unrealistically pessimistic that treatment or anything else will ever make a difference. Thus, the support of loved ones and their encouragement in getting the sufferer to take prescribed medication and to follow through on counseling can be crucial to the success of the treatment.

Whether a particular abnormally depressed person will respond best to counseling alone, medication alone, or both is best decided by a mental health professional. Most psychiatrists and other physicians who prescribe medication do not also do much counseling. Most mental health professionals who provide counseling (psychologists, psychiatric social workers, marriage and family counselors, and some psychiatrists) do not prescribe medication. Thus, it is common for a counselor and a physician to coordinate efforts in treating an abnormally depressed person who needs both counseling and medication.

Frequently, the counselor sees the abnormally depressed person before determining the advisability of referring the individual to a psychiatrist for a simultaneous medication evaluation. Sometimes the abnormally depressed person first sees a physician who recommends counseling.

That abnormal depression is common cannot be denied. Kline believed the following well-known persons suffered from it: Nebuchadnezzar, Saul, Herod, Dostoevski, Poe, Hawthorne, Charles Darwin, Winston Churchill, George Washington, Abraham Lincoln, Thomas Eagleton (vice-presidential candidate), Astronaut Aldrin, and Sigmund Freud.[19]

We should not be surprised at the frequency of the temptation to believe critical tapes or to succumb to irrationally and unrealistically negativistic thinking. The Apostle Paul reminds us:

> No temptation has overtaken you but such as is common to man; and God is faithful, who will not allow you to be tempted beyond what you are able, but with the temptation will provide the way of escape also, that you may be able to endure it. (1 Corinthians 10:13)

I hope this chapter has helped those suffering from abnormal depression to know that they are not alone and that healing "ways of escape" are available.

## Summing It Up

The checklist of symptoms and examples of irrationally and unrealistically negative thinking should help you know whether you suffer from abnormal depression. If you do, the suggestions in this book for dealing with critical tape thinking are for you. You should, however, get a physical examination from your doctor to determine whether your depression is actually a physical problem that should be medically treated. Also, don't hesitate to seek professional Christian counseling, if you need it.

One kind of abnormal depression that deserves attention in its own right is depression brought on by critical tapes that say we are unworthy when we disobey our consciences. This sort of abnormal depression is typically called "guilt."

Do the Scriptures encourage us to replay our critical tapes to ourselves when we sin? Should we lower our self-esteem, fear loss of God's love, or expect punishment—or catastrophe—when we do what is wrong? The next two chapters tell why the Scriptures say no to these questions and how we can respond to our own wrongdoings constructively.

## Target Questions

1. Review the list of symptoms of abnormal depression. (Some of these may occur in severe normal depression.) Have you ever experienced any of these? Which ones? What was happening in your life at the time? Were you replaying any critical tapes?

2. Reread the examples of the schoolteacher's dysfunctional thinking. Have you ever experienced thoughts like those? When? What would have been a more rational and realistic way of thinking? (Refer to the examples of rational and realistic alternatives to the teacher's thinking to help you answer.)

3. If you have been able to recall a time you were engaged in dysfunctional thinking, design a test that might have helped

you realize such thinking was unrealistic or illogical. (Feel free to use ideas suggested in the chapter section.)

4. In your opinion, which biblical passage below best illustrates which example of dysfunctional thinking?

____ *Numbers 13:30–14:11* (Israelites)
____ *1 Samuel 18:6-9* (King Saul)
____ *1 Corinthians 12:14-16* (members of the body of Christ)

A. Since someone has passed me up in one way, that means he will pass me up in other ways in the future, and that means I will lose everything I have (catastrophic thinking).

B. Since I don't have one ability (that another person in my group has), I am completely incompetent and don't belong to the group at all (all-or-nothing dichotomous thinking).

C. We are incapable of doing God's will now and always will be incapable. Even God's promise can't change that (invariant thinking).

5. Did you see yourself in the description of the person who does not exercise his or her God-created capacities to think, feel, and choose as a unique individual? Do you feel like a "nonperson" without a solid core or functioning inner self? If so, in what ways are you not activating your own personality? Why? What do you fear would happen if you changed? What would you like to do differently?

6. Imagine that your Christian friend is abnormally depressed. She has sought professional help, and the counselor has recommended she see a physician for an evaluation to determine whether medication is needed. After the physician recommends medication, your friend is afraid to take it. Her objections? Taking the medication would show lack

of faith and just be a crutch instead of a solution. Besides, she thinks, nothing is really going to help her anyway. What is your advice to her? Why?

7. If you have seldom or never experienced any of the types of normal or abnormal depression described in chapters 8 and 9, review the section in chapter 8 called "Avoiding Depression." Do you see yourself described by any of the examples of how people avoid unpleasant but realistic feelings? Do you see some disadvantages in a pain-free life? Are you willing to begin acknowledging *all* your feelings – pleasant or not?

8. Based on your reading of this chapter and/or your responses to the application exercises, have you made any decisions to do something about changing the way you handle depression? If so, open up your decision to the Lord now. Share with him all your thoughts and feelings about the change(s) you want to make, and ask him to guide and empower you to progress.

# 10
# How Do I
# Handle My Guilt?

In his book, *Whatever Became of Sin?* Dr. Karl Menninger reported the following incident.[1]

> On a sunny day in September, 1972, a stern-faced, plainly dressed man could be seen standing still on a street corner in the busy Chicago Loop. As pedestrians hurried by on their way to lunch or business, he would solemnly lift his right arm, and pointing to the person nearest him, intone loudly the single word "Guilty!"
>
> Then, without any change of expression, he would resume his stiff stance for a few moments before repeating the gesture. Then, again, the inexorable raising of his arm, the pointing, and the solemn pronouncing of the one word "GUILTY!"
>
> The effect of this strange j'accuse pantomine on the passing strangers was extraordinary, almost eerie. They would stare at him, hesitate, look away, look at each other, and then at him again; then hurriedly continue on their ways.
>
> One man, turning to another who was my informant, exclaimed: "But how did he know?"
>
> No doubt many others had similar thoughts. How did he know, indeed?
>
> "Guilty!" Everyone guilty? Guilty of what? Guilty of overparking? Guilty of lying? Guilty of arrogance and hubris toward the one God? Guilty of "borrowing," not to say embezzling? Guilty of unfaithfulness to a faithful wife?

*Guilty only of evil thoughts – or evil plans?*

*Guilty before whom? Is a police officer following? Did anyone see? Will they be likely to notice it? Does he know about it? But that isn't technically illegal, is it?*

*I can make it up. I will give it back. I'll apologize. I wasn't myself when I did that. No one knows about it. But I'm going to quit. It's a dangerous habit. I wouldn't want the children to see me. How can I ever straighten it out? What's done can't be undone.*

Is everyone guilty? Yes. All of us are. And we may experience some painful feelings when we have done what we know is wrong.

As we address guilt in this chapter and the next, I will be adopting the very helpful viewpoint of Dr. Bruce Narramore and Dr. William Counts represented in *Guilt and Freedom.*[2] We are going to look at two kinds of guilt feelings.

Before we can feel guilty, though, we must first have some standards that we believe we should live up to.

## Our Ideals
We all have a picture of the ideal self we would like to be. The ideals or standards toward which we feel we should strive are learned from various sources, such as the Scriptures, church, family and friends, our government, formal education, and the mass media (television, movies, advertisements).

Our ideals may not always be so good from God's perspective, as one woman experienced.

When she went out with a man who made advances toward her, she found herself unable to say no for fear this man would look down on her as "inhibited" or "prudish." She would have felt guilt for *not* commiting fornication.

Her morality was immoral in God's eyes. She could not afford to follow her conscience. It needed to be reformed.

A healthy moral system includes an ongoing process of revision and improvement of the ideal self. Then, according to Dr. Sidney Jourard, one should bless oneself by conforming one's real self to one's ideal self.[3] As we know, the ideal to which God wants to help us conform is the full restoration of what he created and intended each of us to be as images of God.

In this lifetime, we will never be perfect according to God's ideal or our own (unless our own ideal is quite low).

A part of each of us is what the Apostle Paul calls the "conscience." It evaluates how well the real self is measuring up to the ideal self. Christians and non-Christians alike have such a conscience:

> For when Gentiles who do not have the Law do instinctively the things of the Law, these, not having the Law are a law to themselves, in that they show the work of the Law written in their hearts, their conscience bearing witness, and their thoughts alternately accusing or else defending them. . . . (Romans 2:14-15)

In other words, there is an inner guidance system that tells how much on or off course we are at any given moment. Failure to be what we believe we ought to be is likely to result in guilt feelings.

## Guilt Feelings

What do you feel after doing something wrong?
♦ Do you fear God will punish you?
♦ Do you worry about what others may think?
♦ Do you beat yourself by replaying your critical tapes and attacking your self-esteem?

If we do any of these, we become abnormally depressed and engage in dysfunctional thinking. If we are honest, we realize that all of us struggle with such reactions at times.

These reactions are miserable, aren't they? I call them "critical tape guilt."

By contrast, how often do you react to your own sins by loving self-forgiveness, loving self-correction, and loving concern for the consequences to others? We may call this

173

loving type of response "godly sorrow" or "constructive sorrow."

How we respond to ourselves after wrongdoing usually is closely related to how our parents and other significant people (teachers, pastors, brothers and sisters, friends) responded to us when we did wrong as children. We will insist upon correcting ourselves honestly, fairly, and lovingly to the degree that our parents (and others) corrected us assertively, but in love with respect for our integrity.

If we were corrected aggressively or in a manner disrespectful of our feelings or values, we most likely learned to correct ourselves harshly, excessively, and unmercifully. Still, any emotional reaction to falling short may be considered a type of guilt feeling.

Feelings of guilt stemming from critical tapes (self-aggression) are meant to motivate us to obey our standard by fear of lowered self-esteem, fear of losing someone else's love or approval, or fear of punishment. Fear is the taskmaster.

Godly sorrow, by contrast, motivates us by love – loving concern for how our wrong actions result in natural consequences that harm someone and self-forgiveness based on God's loving forgiveness.

## Guilt from Critical Tapes
Let's look at three types of guilt tapes.

*Fear of Punishment.* Fear of punishment is likely to be our most frequent guilt response if, in childhood, we were trained by unnecessary or excessive punishment. Hostile discipline creates critical tape messages that when we do wrong, we are terrible people and deserve to fear that "something frightening will happen."

A boy was often beaten by his alcoholic father who would say, "You'll be the death of me yet." He often rebelled against his unfair and unkind father, getting himself into more trouble. When the boy was twelve, his father died of cirrhosis of the liver. The lad believed his misbehavior was responsible for his father's drinking, abusive behavior, and death. Having been severely and unnecessarily punished so frequently, he expected that he would one day pay for misbehaving and "killing" his father. His critical tape said he was an exceedingly terrible and unworthy person.

Some years later, he married and conceived a child, but his wife developed complications that endangered her own life and that of the unborn child. Labor was induced, and the premature baby was not expected to live. At a time when he needed to cope with depressing circumstances and emotionally support his wife, he was overcome with the expectation that God would take his child to punish him for his father's death.

Abnormal depression in the form of self-induced fear of punishment came to full bloom. He became obsessed with catastrophic horror stories that he imagined would surely depict what would happen to his wife and child. Excessive and cruel punishment programmed him for guilt tapes, abnormal depression, and dysfunctional thinking.

*Fear of the Loss of Love.* Loss of love or approval may be what we fear, especially if we were disciplined by threat of rejection. Then our critical tapes may say, "When you do wrong, Mommy doesn't love you," or "God doesn't love you." The message might be conveyed nonverbally, as when a child is sent to his room but with an angry, unspoken message of rejection so that the child feels excommunicated from the parent. By various means, we might come to fear what others will think.

Carol feared loss of love or approval. After holding her new secretarial job for a full year, she was as nervous as the day she began. So fearful was she of displeasing her boss that she did the work of one and a half people. Her work reviews were always well above average. However, whenever her boss's expression was neutral, not smiling, she felt guilty. She was sure she had lost his approval.

She often succumbed to all-or-nothing dysfunctional

thinking: "Either I am totally capable and my boss approves of me totally, or I am totally incapable and my boss disapproves of me totally. Since his expression is not totally approving he must be totally displeased."

In her girlhood family, nothing she had done ever seemed good enough to her parents or older brothers and sisters. Like the donkey with the proverbial carrot dangled before him that he can never reach, she had worked endlessly for the approval that had never been awarded to her. Her frequent, lifelong inner feeling was "How is it that I'm not good enough for you?" If she ever made a mistake, her guilt feeling was fear that others would reject her.

I used to fear that when I sinned, God was angry with me and loved me less at that moment. I believed his fellowship with me was broken because he could not look at sin. Consequently, when I did sin, I thought I could not ask God to help me out of the mess I had created. It was my own fault, and I had separated myself from him, I supposed.

What relief and exhilarating freedom I experienced when I realized the breadth of God's grace. I did not obtain a relationship with God by good works or obedience in the first place. How could I maintain the relationship by works either? Fellowship with God was, is, and always will be based on *his* loving grace — not on my worthiness measured by my own performance.

Jesus told the parable of the prodigal son to show our heavenly Father's reaction to his erring spiritual children. In the parable, the father never was out of fellowship with his son as far as the father was concerned. He loved him and longed for his return. At no time did he show anger or rejection of any kind for his son. He did, however, reprove the older, faithful son who resented this loving mercy and considered it unfair.

God never stops relating to us. We're the ones who stop relating to him. Repentance is our pivotal movement back to our own intimate, conscious act of relating to our eternally loving God.

*Fear of Lowered Self-Esteem.* Another possible guilt response is that we might fear lowered self-esteem, especially if we were disciplined with shaming or "verbal lashings" that said in effect, "Now don't you feel like a terrible person? Aren't you ashamed of yourself?"

One man recalled he had been disciplined by being sent to his room to think about what he had done. He believed that meant he should think about his critical tapes that said how rotten he was for his actions. He would absorb himself in dysfunctional thinking, attacking his entire character and worth rather than objectively seeing the natural consequences of his behavior that had made it wrong. The time he had to spend thinking this way depended on the severity of his disobedience. The "sentence" varied with the "crime."

As a grown man, he found that he had an internal, fixed schedule for self-loathing. If he spoke harshly to his wife, he had to feel like a terrible person for an hour, and if he made a fool of himself on the job, he would deprecate himself for three to five days. That, by the way, made it more difficult for him to do better on the job. (We also have an indication of his values hierarchy!) In this way, he suffered lowered self-esteem when he did wrong, and he would try to do what was right out of fear of dreaded lower self-esteem.

Another woman tormented by self-beatings reported, "Every time I go to the market, when it comes time to sign my check at the cash register, I feel so guilty that I can't sign my name. I don't know why."

Her parents had accused her frequently and inappropriately of "bad" actions. Shame was continually drilled into her for behavior that was not truly shameful. No matter what she did, she suspected there might be some reason she should be ashamed of it. Daily, she replayed their critical message.

A moment ago, we talked about Christians who supposed God loves them less when they sin. However, sometimes Christians love themselves less at those times. Many Christians even think that when they feel rotten and unlovable, it is the Holy Spirit convicting them. But nowhere do the Scriptures tell Christians to reject themselves for sinning. God does not stop loving us when we sin (Romans 5:8). Who are we to do differently!

## Do Guilt Tapes Work?

Critical tapes in the form of fear of punishment, fear of loss of love, or fear of lowered self-esteem may lead us to live up to our standards, but at what a price psychologically. Going through this sort of mental torture, punishment, and misery is too high a price. We may project onto God that he is "the Great Policeman in the Sky" who is going to "get" or punish us. Or we may fear he will withdraw his love. Or perhaps we will believe the Holy Spirit will "convict" us by causing us to think less of ourselves. These are all destructive reactions.

I was amazed to read an article reprinted by the United States Printing Office that tended to define guilt as fear motivating one to do what is right. It said that guilt

> *is a civilizing force that, when unbridled, can cause much hurt. But with wisdom fortified by knowledge, this pervasive emotion can be tamed and used to your advantage as you go on with the business of living.*[4]

*Guilt Tapes Are Selfish.* Does this sort of guilt really work? The problem is that it is self-centered. Look at all of these concerns about myself: "How am I going to get it now?" "What will people think of me?" "I hate myself!" None of these is a concern for what I have done to someone else.

Let's take an example from Adam and Eve. Although their disobedience in the Garden of Eden altered the spiritual condition of themselves and the entire human race, this tragedy was not their concern. They were afraid of punishment only when God came down and confronted them.

The motive caused by guilt tapes is to avoid bad feelings: fear of what others will think of us, fear of what we will think of ourselves, or fear of getting caught. We may then conform out of duty, but there is no joy in it. It is not from our hearts.

Suppose you and I were to have coffee together, and I spilled my coffee on you. I could fear that you were purposely going to spill your coffee on me to get even. That would be fear of punishment. I could say, "You must think I'm a real stooge!" That would be fear that you will dislike me or look down on me. Or I could say, "Oh! what a stupid idiot I am! Am I embarrassed!" That would be lowered self-esteem.

All these responses would be fear reactions, and all would be self-centered.

By contrast, I could be genuinely concerned for you and quickly gather some paper towels to help you clean up. I could also offer to pay your cleaning bill. Those responses would stem from an unselfish, loving attitude that self-centered fear does not produce.

*Guilt Tapes Misunderstand Grace.* Another problem with fear as a response to wrongdoing is that it indicates a lack of faith. Since Jesus already took all the punishment necessary for our sins, why do we punish ourselves for our wrongs by thinking less of ourselves, expecting others to stop loving us, or dreading catastrophe? Why do we feel we still have to do penance?

Betty had done penance for years because of a serious mistake she had made. She and Ray had begun dating as college students. Unfortunately, they found themselves "in a family way," with their wedding following. Soon after came the baby and marital discord, all under the roof of her parents' house. Family life became, not a dream come true, but a nightmare.

Betty blamed herself for having seduced Ray in the first place. Now whatever immaturity or selfishness he dished out, she would take as her due. God was punishing her for her sin, she thought. However, after twenty-five years of misery, she decided she had paid for her sins in full. She became bitter over all that she had allowed Ray to dump on her. Had she forgiven herself instead of enduring the mental torture of her own guilt tapes, she probably would have communicated more openly with Ray about their relationship, instead of accepting their problems as her way of paying her debt to him and God.

How many of us do penance to God by inflicting guilt tapes on ourselves! As Betty did penance to Ray, we may do penance to God. As the man who thought he had to feel like a rotten person for a specified period of time before he could forgive himself, we may think we have to "feel sorry," by which we may unfortunately mean "feel like a terrible and unlovable person" (rather than "feel concern for the consequences to others"). We may force ourselves to feel terrible for an extended time to persuade God to forgive us.

It should be enough to know that Jesus is the "propitiation" for our sins (1 John 2:2 and 4:10). In appeasing God's wrath, he satisfied God's justice, and that is sufficient to handle our sin. Hebrews 10 says Jesus' death was the sacrifice for our sins for *all* time. No other punishment or sacrifice for sin is necessary: "By this will we have been sanctified through the offering of the body of Jesus Christ once for all. . . . For by one offering He has perfected for all time those who are sanctified" (Hebrews 10:10, 14).

What guilt tapes show is our lack of faith in Christ's finished, completed work on the cross. When we indulge in mental torment or replaying old critical tapes, we are saying that Jesus may not know it, but he did not suffer enough to pay adequately for our sins. We are going to "help" him out. That is, we are going to do penance and add to the work of the cross.

*Guilt Tapes Are Based on Law, Not on Grace.* The sort of critical tape guilt feelings that are characterized by fear may be consistent with the law in the Old Testament, but not with grace in both the Old and New Testaments. The law says, "If I perform, I am accepted." God's grace says, "I am loved and accepted. Therefore, I want to perform."

Does the Bible say we should fear when we sin? Non-Christians have reason to fear. But not once are God's spiritual children taught to fear punishment, expect loss of God's love, or lower their self-esteem.

The following chart shows that non-Christians should fear eternal, spiritual death or everlasting contempt as punishment for sin. For Christians, this punishment is also deserved, but has lovingly been paid in full by Jesus. Therefore, we are no longer under God's condemnation (Romans 8:1).

## GUILT TAPES ARE BASED ON LAW, NOT GRACE

| Under Law (Non-Christians) | | Under Grace (Christians) | |
|---|---|---|---|
| **Fear Punishment?** | | | |
| | | Sins Paid For | Hebrews 10:10,14 |
| Eternal Death | Romans 6:23 | No Condemnation | Romans 8:1 |
| Eternal Contempt | Daniel 12:2 | Loving Discipline | Hebrews 12 |
| **Fear Loss of Love?** | | | |
| God's Wrath | John 3:36 | God's Acceptance | Romans 5:8; 8:38-39 |
| Men-Pleasers | Matthew 6:16 | Not Men-Pleasers | Ephesians 6:6-7 |
| **Lower Self-Esteem?** | | | |
| Worthless | Romans 3:10-12 | Righteous | 2 Corinthians 5:21 |

The Scriptures distinguish between God's discipline and his punishment. Discipline is for his spiritual children (Hebrews 12:5-13), while punishment is for those who have rejected forgiveness and membership in God's spiritual family (Romans 6:23, Daniel 12:2, Hebrews 9:27). Punishment always takes the form of negative consequences, but discipline may take different forms, including negative or positive consequences or other forms of instruction.

The purpose of God's discipline is to train his children to live up to his ideals so that their joy may be complete. The purpose of punishment, however, is to pass judgment or to sentence someone to pay for his or her wrongdoing. Punishment is motivated by anger, but discipline is motivated by love. God never punishes Christians because he punished Jesus in their place and thereby satisfied his anger.

What about the loss of love? While all of us deserve to be rejected by God and subjected to his wrath, only unbelievers will actually experience this. They should fear it; believers should not. The Scriptures totally assure us God loves and has forgiven us and nothing can separate us from his love (Romans 5:8; 8:38-39). Our sins will not cause us to lose God's love. Furthermore, we should not live primarily to please other people and win their approval, but we should do God's will from our hearts because we want to (Matthew 6:1-6; Ephesians 6:6-7). This means a dramatic shift in motive from fear to "want to."

As for lowered self-esteem, we should be well aware by now that, though the Scriptures say sin has made each of us morally worthless, this problem has been remedied by Christ. When God put our moral worthlessness on Jesus and punished him for it, he lovingly took Jesus' moral perfection at the same time and credited it to everyone who comes to Christ for forgiveness.

The wonderful news of Scripture is that even when we deserve to think less of ourselves or when we fear rejection or punishment, we do not have to. In fact, we should not do it[5] because God accepts us. This acceptance is not based on how well we keep his law, but on his own saving, unchangeable grace.

## Behavioral Outcomes of Guilt Tapes
A guilt response to critical-tape guilt is not only selfish and unscriptural, but also ineffective in motivating genuine obedience. What guilt produces is outward conformity or downright rebellion.

*Outward Conformity*. The fear motive can make us outwardly do the right thing, but it cannot make us want to from the heart. It can only produce a veneer of goodness.

A couple bought a bedroom set that was supposed to be solid walnut. After they had owned it a year, however, the veneer began chipping off. It was not on the inside what it was on the outside.

Perhaps the greatest hindrance to personal growth and the spread of Christianity is the conformity veneer of Christians. Probably all of us are hypocritical at least sometimes, aren't we? Our veneer of outward conformity can be seen for what it is.

Many non-Christians also have veneer righteousness. They look like good people as people go, but on the inside they do not obey out of loving God and his ways from the heart. However, I believe there are also non-Christians who, due to a loving upbringing or other helpful experiences, do strive to base their moral code on what will produce desirable natural consequences for others and themselves. No one is perfect.

As a Christian adolescent, I was in a youth group that taught that we should lead morally clean lives. Some of the reasons given for doing so were scriptural, and some were based on a type of fear motivation, or critical tape thinking: "If you are immoral, you should think less of yourself or fear what others will think of you." Some of us did live up to scriptural, moral standards, but not from our hearts. What the other teenagers were doing looked like fun. We would have loved to engage in sin, but we were just too scared to. That was outward conformity.

One of the most dramatic scriptural examples of outward conformity was the Pharisees. They were a group of religious leaders who were masters at how to get around the whole point of God's Law while obeying it technically. To all appearances, their moral performance was flawless. They worked hard at making the correct impression. They ran in the right circles and were seen doing the right deeds at the right places. Jesus saw through them. He said,

*Woe to you, scribes and Pharisees, hypocrites! For you clean the outside of the cup and of the dish, but inside they are full of robbery and self-indulgence. You blind Pharisees, first clean the inside of the cup and of the dish, so that the outside of it may become clean also.* (Matthew 23:25-26)

If we are honest, don't we see a little Pharisee in ourselves, too?

*Rebellion.* An outward conformist may at times be a frustrated rebel like the child who is told, "Sit down!" and who answers, "I may be sitting down on the outside, but I'm standing up on the inside!"

Most people dislike and even resent being motivated by fear or critical tapes. While the outward conformist tries to avoid the feared mental torment (meanwhile inwardly rebelling), some people simply refuse to accept fear motivation and straightforwardly rebel.

We are told in Scripture that Adam and Eve rebelled against God's law and the fear of its forewarnings of punishment. As you may recall, God told Adam and Eve they could eat of any tree of the Garden but one.

When the tempter—the Serpent—came, he said, "Has God said you should not eat of that tree? It's OK. Nothing to fear. In fact, you'll like it if you try it." So they did, thereby revising the standard of what God wanted from them so that they could rationalize committing disobedience.

When God confronted Adam: "Did you eat of that tree?" Adam said in effect, "Eve made me do it. But then again, maybe it's your fault, God, because you gave her to me. Don't blame me. I'm not responsible."

Though they minimized responsibility for their own actions, they did not hypocritically pretend to have left the fruit untouched. They simply out and out rebelled, as we sometimes do. The following contemporary example further illustrates this point.

Nancy had been raised in a strict religious home. She had had to bow to her parents wishes, which they equated with what God wished. To do otherwise meant that God would hurt her. Meanwhile, God was watching her—not to care for her, but to catch her in any sin.

Nancy believed that according to her parents, the worst thing she could possibly do was to say what she really felt or to assertively take care of herself. She should always follow whatever others wished and appear to be the "model child" in appearance, manners, and school grades. If she failed, her punishment was to feel like a selfish, unlovable person and to fear what people would think of her family. It seemed that God loved her "neighbor," but not her. She was systematically taught to submerge her wishes and outwardly conform to the wishes of relatives, family, friends, and her parents.

As a consequence, in her ten years of marriage she deeply felt that every wish of her husband, Ron, had to be her command. After a decade of this, she finally was so embittered that she could no longer be intimidated by fear—fear of guilt and selfishness, fear of anger from others, fear of punishment from God. She told Ron she did not love him.

When she told him that, she seemed ice cold and hardened against how he, the children, or her parents might feel. She moved out. A week later, it came to light that she was having an affair, using cocaine, and experimenting with a very different life-style.

Rebellion frequently involves: (1) revising previous standards or ideals, (2) not accepting responsibility for rebellious behavior, and (3) projecting blame onto someone else. Rebels, like outward conformists, are generally more concerned about getting caught and avoiding punishment than about the destructive consequences of their wrongdoing on others. However, very bitter rebels may accept responsibility for their choices and callously not care about the consequences they may face. Neither outward conformists nor rebels are living by God's standards from the heart.

## Summing It Up

Critical tapes can only inspire outward conformity or rebellion. Fear of punishment, loss of love, or lowered self-esteem when we fall short of our ideals are guilt feelings that are selfish and based on law, not grace. Guilt tapes do not work. *Fear fails.*

What motivation, then, will cause us to be good because we want to with all our inner being? The next chapter answers this question.

## Target Questions

1. This chapter says that as we get to know God's Word better, we can better test our values by his values. Did you ever believe some behavior was wrong, only to find out later that the Scriptures do not label the behavior as wrong? How about the reverse: did you used to believe some behavior was all right, but then discover the Scriptures say it is wrong?

2. When you were disciplined as a child, was it done in any of the following ways? (Check all that apply.) Can you recall specific examples?

   A. Unnecessary, excessive punishment (e.g., beatings, destruction of your possessions, unreasonable restrictions).

   B. Withdrawal of love, silent treatment, threat of rejection, hostile parental attitude.

   C. Shaming, "verbal lashings" that undermined your self-esteem.

   D. Lack of, or inadequate, discipline of any kind.

   E. Lovingly pointing out the consequences of the wrongdoing, lovingly disciplining for the purpose of instruction, and helping you make things right.

3. When you do something wrong, how do you talk to or treat yourself? To answer this, consider these options.

A. Unnecessary, excessive fear of punishment (e.g., dysfunctional thinking in the form of expecting a catastrophe).

B. Actually punishing yourself (e.g., forcing yourself to overeat and gain weight, not allowing yourself to marry a good person, tolerating mistreatment, having an accident, or otherwise doing penance).

C. Fear of others withdrawing love, rejecting you, becoming hostile toward you.

D. Actually getting someone to reject you, because you feel this is what should happen.

E. Shaming and "verbal lashings" toward yourself. Attacking your own self-esteem.

F. Lovingly pointing out to yourself the consequences of your wrongdoing, lovingly instructing yourself to change, and helping yourself think of any possible ways to make things right.

Did anyone benefit from your self-punishment? Did you? Would you intentionally choose to do it again? Compare your answers to questions 2 and 3. Do you think you discipline yourself in a manner that resembles the way your parents disciplined you?

4. Have you ever confronted someone (an adult, a child) who then responded by attacking his or her own self-esteem, fearing what you thought of him or her or fearing punishment, yet who showed no concern for the consequences of the wrongdoing itself to you or to someone else? If so, was that the response you desired? How did you feel? What did you do?

Do you recall ever responding in any of these ways yourself after being confronted by someone? If so, how did the other person then react?

Based on your observations and answers above, would you like to make any changes in yourself?

5.  Reread Hebrews 10:10, 14. Do you believe Jesus satisfied all the punishment that is necessary for God to forgive you and clear you of all guilt? Why or why not?

Have you ever asked God to forgive all your sins, letting Jesus' death count as your punishment for you? If not, would you like to tell God you are taking that step and giving your life to him right now?

If you have already done so, would you like to thank Jesus for his gift of dying for you?

6.  Review the chart on page 181. Do you agree that non-Christians have reason to fear punishment, fear loss of a relationship with God, and fear lowered self-esteem? Why or why not?

Do you agree that Christians, whether they *deserve* to do so or not, *need* not and *should* not engage in such fears? Why or why not?

7.  Can you recall a time you conformed to what was expected of you (by God, parents, teachers, peers, or others) outwardly, but not from your heart? Did you feel like a hypocrite? (Did you fear punishment, someone thinking less of you, or what you would think of yourself?) Why wasn't your conformity from your heart? If you had the incident to live over again, would you handle it differently? If so, how? Why?

8.  Do you recall ever rebelling against the expectations of someone in authority or of peers? Did you change any of your own views of right or wrong to help you decide to rebel? Did you suspect you would be punished or thought less of by others or yourself? If so, did you care? Why or why not?

Were there any natural consequences of your rebellious actions that turned out to be potentially or actually harmful to someone? If you had the situation to handle over again, would you do it any differently? If so, how?

9. Is there some area of temptation or disobedience in your life that you can't seem to overcome, some area where your thoughts exclude Jesus as your Lord? Do you wish God would help you want to do what is right with your whole heart? If so, you may wish to make this request known to God in prayer. Thank him in advance for his answer. Also, look for helpful suggestions in the next chapter.

Consider following this admonition to "confess your sins to one another, and pray for one another, so that you may be healed. The effective prayer of a righteous man can accomplish much" (James 5:16). Sharing your need with a prayer partner, an understanding small group fellowship, a trusted friend, or even a pastor or counselor may be options you would like to consider.

# 11
# How Do I
# Unload My Guilt?

An American tourist drove a rented Volkswagen bus from Germany to Turkey and rendezvoused in Istanbul with two friends in separate cars during the thick of the evening rush hour. Leading them caravanstyle through town and spotting an accident ahead that was beginning to block traffic, he quickly made a right turn down a short, momentarily empty, one-way street going the wrong way. Then immediately, he turned again down a different main route to look for the restaurant that was their destination.

The other two American drivers behind him who were part of his party saw him solve the traffic problem by darting down the short one-way road, which they both saw went the wrong direction. Neverthless, they each rationalized that the first driver had thought it was all right and had made it without mishap. They followed and were pulled over by the police.

One driver went into hysterics. "You won't throw me in prison, will you?" He wrung his hands and berated himself for his own stupidity.

The other driver who had been stopped remained rational but concerned. He walked up to the panicking driver and said, "Look! We could have killed someone. Did you think about that? Now your hysteria may make things worse for both of us. Calm down so we can figure our way through this mess!"

After they both got traffic tickets, they met as originally

planned for dinner and found the first driver, who was baffled as to why the other two had taken so long to get to the restaurant. He had never noticed the sign warning him that his shortcut was a one-way road going the wrong way!

All three drivers had been guilty of breaking the law, yet each had reacted differently. One had been ignorant of his wrongdoing, evidencing no emotional reaction at all. Another had been merely concerned about going to prison and inflicted guilt tapes on himself. Only the third one manifested true concern for the consequences to others as well as to himself. These men illustrate different types of guilt.

## Four Kinds of Guilt

In the previous chapter, I pointed out two types of *guilt feelings*: guilt tapes and godly sorrow. However, there are at least four types of guilt. Two of them are types of feelings, while two are not.

*Civil Guilt.* First, there is civil guilt. The government legislates laws, and if I disobey them, I am guilty of breaking the civil law. Feelings may or may not be connected with this type of guilt. I may be driving over the speed limit and not even realize it, or I may not care.

Civil guilt is merely an objective, judicial, legal fact. It really has little to do with feelings. The first driver in the opening vignette of this chapter illustrates civil guilt.

*Theological Guilt.* The second type of guilt, theological guilt, is the breaking of God's law. As with civil guilt, I may or may not have any feelings about my theological guilt at all! It is an objective fact to which the Scriptures refer. For example, consider James 2:10: "For whoever keeps the whole law and yet stumbles in one point, he has become guilty of all." Jesus is talking about points of the law, not feelings.

Let's look at Jesus' words in Matthew 5:22: "But I say to you that everyone who is angry with his brother [he seems to be talking about aggression] shall be guilty before the court."

*Court* is a common legal term. "And whoever shall say to his brother, 'Raca' [the Aramaic term for *empty-headed* or *good-for-nothing*], shall be guilty before [or liable to] the supreme court."

In Jesus' time the Jews had a religious court that would try certain types of cases. This is the court to which Jesus is referring. "And whoever shall say, 'You fool,' shall be guilty enough to go into the fiery hell." All of these terms are referring to points of the law, law-breaking, and penal consequences (or punishment). Emotions are beside the point. It may happen that, as we read these passages, we will begin to have some feelings, but feelings are not the issue. Theological guilt is a factual, objective, judicial sort of thing.

The New Testament has three words that are translated into the English word *guilt*. The first means "liable to a charge or action at law."[1] The second means "brought to trial" or literally, "under judgment,"[2] while the third means "to owe or be indebted, especially financially."[3] In Jesus' day, if you ran up a debt and did not pay it, you incurred legal liability punishable by imprisonment. All of these words for *guilt* are judicial terms, not terms for feelings.

This finding comes as a surprise to many Christians, and it explains why Christian theologians and psychologists often clash when they attempt to dialogue about guilt. They are usually referring to different things by the same term. That is, theologians accurately use the term *guilt* to mean the state of having broken God's law. Psychologists, however, use the word *guilt* to mean what we are here calling guilt tapes.

Understanding these two different uses of *guilt*, we can see why theologians become upset at psychologists who say they want to free people of the notion of *guilt*, while psychologists are alarmed when theologians fight to retain "guilt" as necessary and valid. When the confusion is cleared up, we discover that both theologians and psychologists want people to find freedom from guilt tapes, and both psychologists and theologians recognize people are judicially guilty of breaking laws.

*Critical Tape Guilt.* While civil and theological guilt are the two objective types of guilt, there are also two types of guilt feelings. One is guilt stemming from critical tapes, which we have discussed and which was illustrated by the second driver in the story leading this chapter.

Some people think that when we do wrong, God expects us to feel some sort of misery over ourselves. However, as we have already indicated, not once are Christians commanded to fear punishment, to lower their self-esteem, or to fear rejection. It cannot be overemphasized that God does not convict us by making us feel fears of this kind. The Holy Spirit is not one of our critical persons.

*Godly Sorrow.* The other type of guilt feeling is godly sorrow. Constructive in nature, it is concern for the natural consequences of our wrongdoings and is synonymous with true repentance. It, then, is God's alternative to guilt tapes. The third driver in the opening story of this chapter illustrates constructive sorrow. The Holy Spirit will help us respond with godly sorrow as we learn more about it and cooperate with him.

### Love and Reason

We are better able to respond to our sins with godly sorrow when we understand the real reason sin is wrong.

I asked a teenager who had stolen makeup from a store whether she thought stealing was wrong. She believed it was. Then I asked her why it was wrong. Her answer was that it was against the law and she would have to live with bad feelings about herself. As I pressed her further, it became apparent that she did not know why the state makes and enforces laws against stealing. She certainly did not think she had hurt the store owner or anyone else.

I, therefore, explained how stealing causes the owner to lose the money he spent to stock the store with goods, that it lessens his ability to support his family and the families of his employees. It also forces him to raise prices so that all the customers end up having to pay for the losses from stealing. When she understood that stealing has natural consequences that hurt others, she felt genuine regret from her heart and made restitution to the store manager.

The reason God forbids certain actions is not because he enjoys sitting in an ivory tower someplace and concocting whimsical ways to restrict us. Certain actions or attitudes are wrong, because they result in natural consequences that are harmful to ourselves or others.

As we saw in an earlier chapter, the Psalmist says of God's laws, "Moreover, by them Thy servant is warned; in keeping them there is great reward" (Psalm 19:11). God's guidelines warn us away from needlessly harmful actions and direct us to ways of living that are fulfilling and satisfying.

God gives us the law because he loves us. If, in turn, we love God and others, we can fulfill the law. Someone asked Jesus,

> *"Teacher, which is the great commandment in the Law?" And He said to him, " 'You shall love the Lord your God with all your heart, and with all your soul, and with all your mind.'*
>
> *"This is the great and foremost commandment. The second is like it, 'You shall love your neighbor as yourself.' On these two commandments depend the whole Law and the Prophets." (Matthew 22:36-40)*

All of God's law can be summed up in one word: *love.* Wholesome morality is based on love.

Sins are actions or attitudes that naturally result in unloving consequences to God or humans. We may experience a great deal of pain as a result of sin. If so, this is our own doing and it is regrettable. However, there need be no fear of losing the love of God, nor fear of punishment. Jesus has paid for our sins once and for all, bestowing unchangeable worth on us. He has ended our reason to fear him.

Why, then, should we live by God's ideals? It is because we understand there are reasons for them and because we are motivated by love.

*Applying God's Forgiveness.* First John 1:9 says, "If we confess our sins, He is faithful and righteous to forgive us our sins and to cleanse us from all unrighteousness."

God is a forgiving God, and as we realize and accept his forgiveness, we should likewise be able to forgive ourselves. When we do not live up to God's standards, our response toward ourselves should also be that of love and forgiveness. When we realize God loves us and has forgiven us and that we gain nothing by mentally torturing ourselves, we are free to forgive ourselves.

When her second marriage failed, Sharon felt she would carry an impossible weight of guilt: "I had messed up again. I took the burden of the entire marriage failing on myself." She felt like dirt and mentally pounded herself.

Though she had had a religious upbringing, she had never asked God to forgive her sins and make her a member of his spiritual family. I suggested that if she experienced God's cleansing forgiveness, she would be freer to forgive herself. She confessed her sins, particularly those against her husband, and asked God to forgive her.

"Suddenly from nowhere, a feeling of freedom settled through my whole body," she told me. "It was a physical sensation. I felt like God literally reached down and lifted the problem off my shoulders. From that moment, I began going forward. I couldn't before then. The guilt was too heavy."

When she applied God's forgiveness and forgave herself, too, she was free of guilt tapes. The Scriptures say, "There is no fear in love; but perfect love casts out fear, because fear involves punishment, and the one who fears is not perfected in love" (1 John 4:18). When we understand God's love and forgiveness, we no longer fear punishment from him or punish ourselves in fear.

*Loving Self-correction.* Thereafter, as Sharon worked on changing herself and on wooing back her estranged husband, she still made some of her old mistakes. If she began mentally berating herself, she got into a bad mood and could not improve until she recognized the guilt tapes and stopped them. However, when she corrected herself lovingly and forgivingly, she progressed much more easily.

Her loving self-correction went something like this: "OK, you did it, and it didn't help. You forgot. This is one to learn on, and you get however many you need. You don't have to do it again. God still loves you, and you're still a lovable person."

God is the perfect teacher, and the Scriptures say he disciplines in love (Hebrews 12). When we want to know how to correct ourselves, who is a better model than God? The goal is to learn to correct ourselves as lovingly as he does. Sharon was learning to do this.

## Concern for Consequences to Others

One of Sharon's biggest problems in her marriage had been her temper and unrelenting self-berating over it. For example, she reported, "If we went to Catalina and any part of my dream for the day did not come true exactly, I'd be disappointed and furious for hours. Then I'd apologize for being such a brat and tell him how terrible and ashamed I felt."

Her husband had derived no benefit or joy from seeing her punish herself and feel like a miserable person. What he longed for, instead, was for her to empathize with how miserable she was making *his* life and ask forgiveness for *that.* Her apologies for being a bad person merely seemed self-centered to him. He had suffered from her abusive yelling and cursing, and then, when he himself needed support to live with this, he had gotten nothing from her. She had seemed unconcerned for him!

Sharon was finally able to change this pattern. Making a concerted effort to put herself into her husband's shoes, she tried to feel what it had been like for him to be married to her. In the process, she experienced a sense of grief for the negative impact she had made on him. Soon after, she shared her feelings, and hoped he would forgive her one day. He did!

Sharon's way of making restitution to him was to ask his forgiveness. There are other means of restitution as well. The teenager who had stolen makeup made restitution by paying the store manager for what she had stolen. The Bible gives examples of persons who experienced God's loving forgiveness and responded with godly sorrow for the consequences of their sins against others. One was Zaccheus, the tax collector (Luke 19:8), who spontaneously wanted to pay back four times the amount he had cheated from taxpayers.

Sometimes, however, it is not wise or prudent to make restitution, for example, when confession may cause more pain to someone who never knew there was a problem. The decision in each case is based on what we believe God would have us do.

*When Restitution Fails.* Suppose we offer restitution, believing this is needed in a given situation for the healing of the consequences of our sin, and it is not accepted. What do we do then?

We may be rejected for several reasons:

1. The person we wronged may feel our motive is not lovingly to undo harm brought upon him or her, but selfishly to free ourselves from guilt feelings.

2. The person may feel we do not yet fully see the extent of our wrong and the consequences, especially emotional pain, we have caused.

3. The other person feels guilty, too, and seeks self-justification by balancing his or her own guilt against ours. By removing our guilt, the other is faced with guilt and may not want to admit to being wrong.

How do we discern the nature of the problem? For one thing we may wish to ask the person directly why our apology or other restitution was rejected. If we sense the other person is at fault and cannot admit it, we may need to try to discover whether that person will respond better to being confronted or to our respecting his or her chosen reaction. Ultimately, we can be responsible only for our own actions, not for the responses of others. All any of us can do is our best. We must leave the rest in God's hands.

## Result: Change from the Heart

The result of loving sorrow for the harmful consequences of unloving actions is change that comes from the heart. It is true repentance. Godly sorrow is the way to get a real strong case of the "want to's."

Sharon changed because she had emerged from her deep hole of guilt tapes. She was free and was able to change because she wanted to. Her husband, who had given her up as a hopeless case, was astonished at the changes she had made in herself during their eight months of separation. Not only that, but he began to feel the love for her that he had believed he would never feel again. The weekend he moved back home, it rained so hard that their swimming pool overflowed and flooded their house. There they were, pulling back the carpets, so happy to be together again—floods and all!

The Apostle Paul recorded an instance of godly sorrow in the first-century church at Corinth. A man had been sleeping with his father's wife, which must have meant his stepmother. Paul said, in effect, "The ungodly don't even do that, and you people aren't concerned. You're acting as though there is nothing wrong with it. You need to lovingly correct this person," and they did. Thereafter, the man truly repented and changed.

Paul was very pleased with how the Corinthian church had responded:

> *I now rejoice, not that you were made sorrowful, but that you were made sorrowful to the point of repentance; for you were*

*made sorrowful according to the will of God, in order that you might not suffer loss in anything through us. For the sorrow that is according to the will of God produces a repentance without regret, leading to salvation; but the sorrow of the world produces death.*

*For behold what earnestness this very thing, this godly sorrow, has produced in you: what vindication* [vindication *means "clearing" of theological guilt*] *of yourselves, what indignation, what fear* [fear *means "reverential respect"*], *what longing, what zeal, what avenging of wrong! In everything you demonstrated yourself to be innocent in the matter.* (2 Corinthians 7:9-11, The New International Version)

The Corinthians responded in godly sorrow and repented from their hearts, thereby reflecting a genuine and complete obedience to the Lord.

## Changing Our Guilt Feelings

How do you change from guilt tape feelings to genuine godly sorrow?

Since we will never be perfect this side of heaven, we will probably always have to work on this process to some extent.

Let's review the steps or ingredients of godly sorrow:

1. Make sure the behavior to which we feel we should conform is in keeping with God's ideals for us.

2. Reason out what are the unloving consequences for the wrong behaviors we wish to change. Let concern for these replace guilt tape fear.

3. Remember God still loves us despite what we have done. Receive God's forgiveness, and forgive ourselves.

4. Correct ourselves lovingly.

5. Undo harm we may have caused others if this is possible and will contribute to healing for them. Most

commonly, this means fully admitting our wrong, expressing compassion for the other person's pain that we caused, and asking forgiveness.

The process of replacing self-punishment with loving self-correction is essential and ordinarily must be repeated whenever we slip back into guilt tapes. This is the same process we have previously described as replacing critical tapes with affirming ones. However, loving self-correction toward change and sometimes restitution are also needed.

The following experience illustrates how to replace guilt tapes with loving self-correction. Marla's preferred style of handling guilt feelings was lowered self-esteem for weight gain. And whenever she was deeply submerged in hating herself for this, her favorite anesthetic was food. Unfortunately, after stuffing herself, she once again hated herself. She was eating her way to greater and greater self-disgust.

When she learned of loving self-correction as the way out, she endeavored to practice it. Each time after overeating, she would lovingly forgive herself and tell herself she had not committed the sin of gluttony for the first time or the last. "Slimness will not give me value. I would be lovable even if I weighed four hundred pounds. . . ."

Eventually, Marla became kind and merciful to herself. Far from serving as an excuse to eat, loving self-correction broke the vicious sin-guilt-sin cycle. She quit overeating. Changing from fearful self-punishment to loving self-correction enabled her to change her destructive habit.

## What Can Parents Do?

If you are a parent, you may be asking, "How can I raise my child to respond to wrongdoing with constructive sorrow rather than guilt tapes?" Though this book is not primarily a guide for parents, I will at least address this question briefly by focusing on what I feel is the key issue: *disciplining children rather than punishing them.*

The differences between discipline and punishment have

previously been described. Parents can learn much by following the example of how our heavenly Father disciplines rather than punishes us. One of the most important goals toward which parents can aim is to discipline in love rather than in anger or aggression. I say *goal* because parents are not perfect.

The ability to discipline lovingly is one of the things for which I will forever bless my mother. Even when she had to discipline me, I always felt she loved me. It was rare, indeed, that I felt she was angry, shaming, or rejecting toward me for anything I did—even though I knew some of my activities had caused her grief. She had a knack for being firm but not attacking, assertive but not aggressive. Consequences for disallowed behaviors were fair and immediate. Her disciplinary measures were not severe, just consistent.

Before disciplining me, she would hold me on her lap and explain in simple terms why the behavior was wrong, why it was important for me not to do it, and why she had to teach me. It was because she loved me. After a spanking, she held and comforted me, assuring me of her abiding love. I grew up with the conviction that there could be no depth of self-degradation to which I could go that would change her love, God's love, or my value. I felt there was inside of me the solid core of a secure self that would outlast anything life could bring my way.

She was not perfect, nor was I, but she showed me the meaning of loving discipline that has become my pattern for loving self-correction and constructive sorrow.

## Summing It Up

In a previous chapter I mentioned the man who had stood on a busy Chicago street corner and had solemnly pointed his finger at those who passed by, all the while intoning the judgment "Guilty!" Are we all guilty?

Guilty of breaking God's law of love—yes. But we are law-breakers who fear no divine punishment! We have received

God's abundant forgiveness and love. Theological guilt is an objective, lawful condition to which we should respond with godly sorrow, not with guilt tapes. The chart on pages 200-201 tells how. We can let go of fear and be motivated by God's love.

As we do so, we may especially wish to be freed of guilt tapes whenever we feel or express a particular negative emotion, which is anger. What is the biblical moral standard for the emotion of anger? Should we fear lowered self-esteem, loss of love, or punishment when we experience anger? How should we resolve anger? The next chapter is dedicated to dealing with these concerns.

## Target Questions

1. Have you ever broken a law without realizing it at the time? For example, did you ever discover you had been speeding or had parked illegally without noticing? Or have you broken such civil laws intentionally with little or no feeling about doing so?

2. Were you aware that the word *guilt* in the New Testament refers to an objective fact of breaking God's law, not to an emotion? What reactions do you have to this idea?

3. Psalm 19:11 is one of the passages of Scripture that explains that God's laws are given as guidelines for good reasons. There are natural consequences of sin that are destructive, while there are rewarding consequences that naturally come from handling life the righteous way. In Matthew 22:36-40, Jesus said love was God's guiding principle behind all his laws.

Read the portion of the Ten Commandments found in Exodus 20:12-17. Try to think of as many loving reasons behind these directions as you can. If you are reading this book with a study group or class, brainstorm together.

4. Read Psalm 32. Can you think of a time you felt like David—weighted down by unconfessed guilt, then freed after you had asked forgiveness from God or someone else? After you knew God or someone else forgave you, was it easier to forgive yourself, too? Why? Was it easier to change after that? Why?

5. Review the section of "Loving Self-Correction." Have you ever corrected yourself in this way? If not, why not? If so, did it help you change?

6. Can you think of a time someone asked your forgiveness, apologized, or offered to make restitution to you? Did you feel like accepting this gesture? What factors affected your response? For example, did the person seem sincere? Did this individual seem to understand fully the harm done to you and feel grieved for *your* sake? Or did you struggle with pride or guilt tapes yourself in the situation?

Now, from the other vantage point, do you recall someone being hesitant to accept an apology or restitution from you? What factors do you think affected that person's response to your gesture?

7. Do you understand the difference between discipline and punishment? If you are not sure, review the paragraph describing this in chapter 10 under the subheading "Guilt Tapes Are Based on Law, not Grace." Also review the section of the past chapter called "What Can Parents Do?" Re-reading "God Is Not Angry with Me" in chapter 5 may also be helpful.

If you are a parent, can you recall a time you disciplined your child and also a time you punished your child? Was there a difference in your child's response?

Try to think of an instance of when you punished yourself with one or more of the three types of guilt tapes (fear of punishment, fear of loss of love, fear of lowered self-esteem). Try to contrast that with an example of a time you lovingly disciplined yourself in an attitude of constructive sorrow (refer to question 5). Was there a difference in your feelings and your motivation to change?

8. Are there some changes you would like to make in your response to yourself when you sin? Would you like to alter the way you discipline your children in some way(s)? Commit these desires to the Lord in prayer. Ask him to help you as you cooperate with the Holy Spirit by faith.

# 12
# IS MY ANGER WRONG?

As Bob poured out the distressing events surrounding his marital separation, I mentioned he seemed angry at his wife. He merely looked puzzled and made no comment.

Driving home from the therapy session, Bob felt a tidal wave of rage surge through him. He spotted a moving van and tried to run it off the freeway! After his arrival at home, the potentially tragic consequences of his action sank in and terrified him. He arranged an emergency counseling appointment the next day where he began to face and to understand the emotion that had bewildered him—his anger.

## What Is Anger?
Anger is a feeling of displeasure resulting from frustration, injury, mistreatment, opposition, or other situations where we feel we have been unjustly treated. It usually results in a desire to put an end to the source of irritation, to fight back, or to do something to restore our sense of justice.

Anger comes in all degrees of intensity.

Mary and Tom Miller were at the breakfast table, heatedly disagreeing about how they should have disciplined their son the day before when he had failed to mow the lawn for the hundredth time.

Tom asked Mary, "Why are you so angry with me?"

Mary slid to the edge of her chair, then with both fists waving, shouted, "I'm not angry! You don't want to see me when I'm angry!"

Mary and Tom were using the term *anger* very differently. To Mary, anger meant only extreme anger. She meant she was not ready to break dishes. Tom used the term *anger* to include various degrees of anger.

When we are only a little angry, we might say we feel irritated, annoyed, aggravated, or provoked. We might describe a medium amount of anger as feeling mad, resentful, indignant, disgusted, exasperated. A great deal of anger might be verbalized as feeling hate, wrath, fury, rage. Since all of these are words for anger, I will use *anger* throughout this chapter to include any of these degrees of anger.

## Christians Do Feel Anger

I once heard a Christian mother tell her fighting sons, "Christians don't get angry." That is not scriptural information, and it may have left the boys with two possible but unfortunate conculsions to draw from her false belief: either they could hypocritically deny they were angry or they could deduce they must not be Christians.

Christians can and do feel all degrees of anger, including hate. The *feeling* of anger and what we actually *do* about it in choosing our behavior are two different matters. I did not always realize this. God himself feels anger, even in the extreme (Proverbs 6:16-19). Since we are created by God in his image, it should be no surprise that we are equipped to experience the same gamut of emotions as the Scriptures indicate God feels (Proverbs 8:13; Ecclesiastes 3:1, 8). I know I certainly have experienced anger in all degrees—from irritation to even hatred.

## The Value of Anger

Anger is an unpleasant, negative emotion. Then, why would God create us with the capacity to feel it? For the same reason he also designed us to be able to experience physical pain. Discomfort of any kind, be it in the form of emotions or physical sensations, serves as a signal to notify us that something is wrong.

208

Suppose while I am cooking I lay my hand on a red-hot burner. I will feel physical pain. That pain is telling me, "May I have your attention, please! Now hear this. This is an emergency. Remove your hand from the stove!"

If I wished, I could decide that I do not like physical pain when I cook, and therefore I might try to excude such experiences from my awareness. Theoretically, I could undergo surgery to sever nerves between my hand and my brain. I would never again experience physical pain when touching the hot burner. Would that be a good solution? Of course not. As miserable as burning sensations are, I *need* the capacity to feel them.

In the same way, negative emotions such as anger provide us with important information. They tell us there is a problem that requires our attention. It would be pleasant in the short run but dangerous in the long run to decide to deny our awareness of anger.

We have already dealt with various negative emotions:

1. *Normal depression* alerts us to a loss of some kind.

2. *Abnormal depression* tells us we are damaging our self-esteem.

3. *Godly sorrow* warns us of the danger of natural negative consequences for doing wrong.

4. *Guilt feelings* stemming from critical tapes inform us we are placing ourselves under a moral system of law, not grace.

Anger, too, serves a purpose — *to make us aware that we believe injustice has been done.* The pain in negative emotions such as anger instinctively motivates us to put an end to the source of the unpleasantness.

## Putting Away Anger

This chapter focuses on how to resolve anger in personal relationships in a way that affirms our self-esteem and that of others. Our "how-to" comes from Ephesians 4:26-32:

*Be angry, and yet do not sin; do not let the sun go down on your anger, and do not give the devil an opportunity.*

209

> Let him who steals steal no longer; but rather let him labor, performing with his own hands what is good, in order that he may have something to share with him who has need.
>
> Let no unwholesome word proceed from your mouth, but only such a word as is good for edification according to the need of the moment, that it may give grace to those who hear.
>
> And do not grieve the Holy Spirit of God, by whom you were sealed for the day of redemption.
>
> Let all bitterness and wrath and anger and clamor and slander be put away from you, along with all malice.
>
> And be kind to one another, tender-hearted, forgiving each other, just as God in Christ also has forgiven you.

The first thing Paul tells us here is to be angry and yet not sin. Clearly, then, feeling anger is not in itself sin. We need not feel guilty for experiencing anger.

But what we choose to do about our anger may be sin. Paul immediately adds that we should resolve our anger as quickly as possible. Why? Because if we do not, in our desire for relief or justice, we might give the devil opportunity to tempt us to take revenge into our own hands.

In the process, we may become a "critical person," using a variety of tactics:

♦ stealing
♦ unwholesome language
♦ bitterness
♦ continued wrath or anger
♦ prolonged shouting ("clamor")
♦ attacking someone's self-esteem or reputation ("slander").

We are, thus, to do away with anger and vengeful acts and instead focus on loving and forgiving each other as Christ has forgiven us our injustices toward him.

In the same chapter, Paul gives us a constructive way to communicate with each other that would seem to be helpful in "putting away" anger. If we go back one verse in our passage in Ephesians 4, we read:

*Therefore, laying aside falsehood, speak truth, each one of you, with his neighbor, for we are members of one another. Be angry, and yet do not sin; do not let the sun go down on your anger. . . .* (Ephesians 4:25-26)

Paul says we should stop lying and instead tell each other the truth, be angry, and do not sin.

The context indicates that the phrase *speak truth* does not refer to telling each other doctrine or reciting the Apostles' Creed together, as valuable as these activities can be. Rather, *speak truth* in this passage means we should be honest, genuine, sincere. We ought to speak our personal truth about what we really think and feel, including our feelings of anger.

Several verses earlier Paul uses a very similar phrase, "speaking the truth in love":

*But speaking the truth in love, we are to grow up in all aspects into Him, who is the head, even Christ, from whom the whole body, being fitted and held together by that which every joint supplies, according to the proper working of each individual part, causes the growth of the body for the building up of itself in love.* (Ephesians 4:15-16)

It is by "speaking the truth in love," Paul says, that we grow into Christian maturity. He adds another ingredient to speaking the truth — we should *say it in love*.

In this one simple phrase *speaking the truth in love*, Paul has summed up what extensive psychological research has verified to be the core, vital ingredient in healing communication. Speaking the truth in love is the best way to resolve anger in personal relationships.[1]

This phrase also points out common mistakes in communication that can hinder us from "putting away" anger. Namely, we might speak the truth but not say it in love. Or we might speak in love but not tell the truth. Or we might neither speak the truth nor say it in love. Let's look at these three common errors before we present the biblical approach of resolving anger by speaking the truth in love.

## Three Communication Failures

*Aggression.* The first common mistake in communicating our anger is to tell the truth about what we feel but not to say it in love. This type of communication is called *aggression*.

Aggression is attacking the other person with our anger in a vengeful way. It is letting the other person "have it" with both barrels and shooting down the individual's self-esteem. Examples of aggression include name calling, a vicious tone of voice, unfair accusations, and playing judge over other people's motives.

Proverbs 29:11 describes aggression, saying, "A fool always loses his temper, but a wise man holds it back." In other words, the aggressive person puts his mouth in motion before he puts his mind in gear. The wise person counts to ten first.

The following imaginary scene illustrates aggression between a husband and wife. As you read it, notice your automatic reactions.

> *Husband:* Dear, you know how we agreed that today you'd do the grocery shopping and I'd do the laundry?
>
> *Wife:* Yes.
>
> *Husband:* Well, I didn't want it to take all day, so I just threw all the light and dark clothes together in one load. Unfortunately, the colors all ran together.
>
> *Wife:* What! You airhead, vegetable brain, imbecile, moron! You *never* think, do you? Do you know what I think of you? You're just a stupid idiot, idiot, idiot! Get out of my sight, slime!

Does this strike you as a godly way to put away anger? Probably not, yet who of us has never been guilty of aggression to some degree?

Let's look at some of the arguments people make for and against aggression:

1. Some aggressors defend themselves by pointing out that they are speaking the truth about their feelings. They argue, "I let people know exactly how I feel, and if they don't like the way I say it, that's tough." The unfortunate problem I find with this defense is that it makes a virtue of bluntness. If done in love it is seen as admirable to be truthful.

2. Another argument sometimes used in favor of aggression is the belief that it will "get the anger out of your system," that is, that this is the way to put away anger. Ann Landers, noted newspaper columnist, promoted this viewpoint when responding to the following letter from one of her readers:

> *Dear Ann: I was shocked at your advice to the mother whose three-year-old had temper tantrums. You suggested that the child be taught to kick the furniture and "get the anger out of his system." I always thought you were a little cuckoo. Now I'm sure.*
>
> *My younger brother used to kick the furniture when he got mad. Mother called it, "Letting off steam." Well, he's 32 years old now and still kicking the furniture—what's left of it, that is. He is also kicking his wife, the cat, the kids, and anything else that gets in his way. Last October he threw the TV set out of the window when his favorite team failed to score and lost the game. (The window was closed at the time.)*
>
> *Why don't you tell mothers that children must be taught to control their anger? This is what separates civilized human beings from savages, Dummy.*
>
> *— Star Witness*
>
> *Dear Star: You, like some others who wrote to criticize, ignored the most important part of my answer. I did not con-*

> *done destroying furniture. I suggested that a punching bag*
> *or an old chair, specifically set aside for the purpose, be the*
> *object of the child's hostility. And P.S. — the most important*
> *part of my answer went like this: "Youngsters should be*
> *taught to vent their anger against things — not people."*[2]

Occasionally, some counselors encourage their counselees to vent their anger on a safe object as a temporary measure. Their purpose is to enable individuals to gain insight into the presence and intensity of their anger until they can express it adequately in words. However, moving on from aggression to assertiveness and forgiveness is the goal. Why?

Because, as popular as this proaggression view may be in some circles, research does not support its effectiveness in putting away anger. In fact, one of the leading psychological researchers on aggression, Berkowitz,[3] found that aggression actually reinforces future aggression, shaping the individual to become habitually aggressive.

Aggression may, at most, allow the aggressor to feel relieved of anger if three conditions exist:

1. The angry person or an acceptable substitute must attack the real person who is seen as the source of the injustice.

2. The aggressor must feel no anxiety (for example, about retaliation).

3. The aggressor must feel no remorse (about hurting someone else in the process).

The moral unacceptability of these conditions on the personal level should be obvious. These conditions would seem to be fulfilled best, in the scriptural view, by authority figures who have been invested with legitimate power to carry out justice (Romans 13:1-8). However, when carried out on a personal level, behaving aggressively is immoral because it means the aggressor must feel no qualms about believing that his or her feelings and self-esteem matter, while the other person's do not.

In an earlier chapter, we discussed reasons why Romans

12:19 declares that aggression is God's job, not ours. Proverbs 24:17-18 also forbids us from taking pleasure in the pain of our enemies when God gives them their just deserts: "Do not rejoice when your enemy falls, and do not let your heart be glad when he stumbles; lest the Lord see it and be displeased, and He turn away His anger from him." There is no room at all for the so-called pleasure of sweet revenge or aggression.

Even when aggression does manage for the moment to put away one person's anger through unholy means, it does not put away the other person's anger. Someone once said, "A sharp tongue is the quickest way to a split lip." Personally, I like the adage, "He who throws mud loses ground."

The victim of aggression may counterattack, fueling the fire and escalating the anger of both people. Or the victim may hold in anger for the moment, only to reopen the case later on. At that time the aggressor may become unfairly angry, saying, "I just got over my anger. Why are you digging up the past? Now I'm getting angry again. Why can't you let the past be over and done?"

Aggression is a win-lose solution to anger. The aggressor wants to win the right to his feelings and is willing for the victims to lose. The victim may not be so willing.

Aggression, by definition, is not loving. The aggressor is being a critical person assaulting the self-esteem of someone who is the image of God. Aggression is attacking God in effigy.

*Passivity.* While aggression is speaking the truth but not saying it in love, passivity is the opposite — speaking in love but not telling the truth. Passivity is bottling up anger inside, possibly not even admitting to feeling it, and repressing or suppressing it. Outwardly, the passive person appears kind.

Let's rerun the same imaginary situation we saw earlier between a husband and wife, this time seeing how anger might be handled passively. Tune into your emotional reactions.

*Husband*: Dear, you know how we agreed that today you'd do the grocery shopping and I'd do the laundry?

*Wife*: Uh, huh.

*Husband*: Well, I didn't want it to take all day, so I just threw all the light and dark clothes together in one load. I'm sorry to say the colors all ran together.

*Wife*: Oh, that's OK.

*Husband*: It is? Well, our little girl's red dress ran on your floor length dress.

*Wife*: Oh, my old one?

*Husband*: No, your expensive new one that your mother gave you on your birthday. You aren't upset, are you?

*Wife*: Oh, no. Why would I be upset?

*Husband*: Well, also, my new jeans ran dark blue on the rest of the dress.

*Wife*: That's all right. I don't mind.

*Husband*: Oh, good. Well, the hook on your skirt also caught on the lace of your other dress and shredded the lace. You aren't mad at me, are you?

*Wife*: No. That's fine.

Do you think this wife is successfully putting away her anger? If you were she, wouldn't you be furious behind that sweet facade?

Why would anyone choose to deal with anger passively?

Unfortunately, many Christians believe passivity is Christian. They do not feel permission to experience or to admit anger. They equate anger with aggression, which they know is sinful.

Some Christians with low self-esteem do not believe their feelings count. I secretly used to believe God loved my neighbor more than he loved me. Thinking I had to be sweet to people no matter how they stabbed me, I allowed them, especially non-Christians I hoped to win to Christ, to wipe their feet on me. I continued doing this even as I observed them losing respect for me and ridiculing me behind my back.

What I was telling them between the lines was "Come to Christ so you, too, can be a doormat who is phoney and miserable and can't take care of herself. This is how Christ equips his believers for victorious living." How sad!

Another motive for being passive is fear of hurting someone and/or getting hurt in retaliation. One woman believed that expressing anger was selfish. Other people's feelings counted, but hers did not. Her critical tapes were "Don't think," "Don't feel," and "Don't talk." In short, they said, "Don't be you."

What motivated her to keep living by this thinking? Fear of feeling like a bad person and fear of losing the love and approval of others. She had let her parents choose her friends, her car, her college, and her career. Then she had let her husband choose her home, her furniture, and her forms of recreation. She had never showed resentment over any of this. Everyone thought hers was the perfect marriage, because there were no apparent conflicts. Her husband thought the relationship was boring but smooth. She had always been agreeable and loving—outwardly. Secretly, he felt he never really knew her, and he resented having to make all the decisions without her input.

To everyone's shock, after fifteen years of marriage, one day she told her husband she did not love him. She heaped her feelings of hostility upon him—fifteen years' worth in one big blow-out.

Passivity is martyrdom. It can be a time bomb for later aggression. When we martyr ourselves by holding in anger, our benefactors eventually may very well become our victims and pay for all our sacrifices — dearly.

Some passive people regularly see-saw between passively saving up anger and aggressively dumping it all at once. While in the saving-up stage, they may, at times, become passive aggressive.

*Passive Aggression.* Passive aggression is outwardly appearing to speak truth in love, while actually doing neither. It is being dishonest and expressing aggression in indirect, sneaky ways.

Consider how our imaginary couple might illustrate passive-aggressive coping with anger. Once again, notice your internal reaction.

> *Husband:* Honey, I put the dark and light clothes together in the same load of laundry because I wanted to hurry. The colors ran together. You aren't upset, are you?

> *Wife:* Oh, no. That's what I've learned to expect from you.

> *Husband:* You have? Oh. Well, your new dress got ruined. You aren't mad at me, are you?

> *Wife:* Why should I be mad? Just because now I won't have a decent dress to wear to *your* parents' anniversary party. Actually, I'm only surprised you didn't wash your wool suit and silk tie in the load too. Did you toss your *brain* in while you were at it? *It* could use some laundering.

Do you feel the sneaky jabs? The wife overtly denies anger but covertly evidences it by sarcastically attacking her husband's self-esteem (specifically, his intelligence). Thus, she gives a confusing double message.

Meanwhile, she never directly addresses the true reason for her anger, namely that she herself resents losing her dress due to his carelessness. If her husband complains, she can point to the actual words she said: "*All I said* was . . ." She

218

then can deny the existence of the messages between the lines by saying, "I was only kidding. Can't you take a joke? You're too sensitive."

Why do some people choose to be passive aggressive? They may fear retaliation if they directly express their anger. Passive aggression allows them to get even without other people being able to pinpoint what is being done to them. Some of these passive aggressors become so adept at this manipulation that their skill at sarcasm may become a source of pride.

In our fictitious illustration, the wife quite consciously used passive aggression in the form of sarcasm. Sometimes, though, passive aggression is done unconsciously:

♦ A woman whose cantankerous father-in-law lived in her home discovered that she had "accidentally forgotten" to feed him dinner for several nights in a row!

♦ Another woman whose husband hated to have his soft-boiled eggs overcooked listened to her exasperated spouse complain that she had "accidently" hard-boiled his eggs every day without fail. The calmer she remained while protesting that she "couldn't help it" since it was a daily "accident," the more frustrated and infuriated he became.

Sometimes passive-aggressive people are amazed at how angry their family members are at them "for no apparent reason."

The passive aggressor, like the aggressor, is being a critical person attacking the other person's self-esteem and feelings. However, like the passive person, the passive aggressor is also hypocritical or deceitful. At best, only part of the truth about anger is communicated. The whole truth is unclear. Also, the approach is not loving.

Passive aggression is the worst of both worlds. Anger is stirred up at least as much as it is put away.

*Assertiveness.* That brings us to the fourth alternative — speaking the truth in love. This ideal approach can be accomplished in two steps: first by oneself, then with the other person.[4]

By speaking the truth in love to oneself I mean meditating on, or thinking through, the anger. Ephesians 4:26 is actually a quote from Psalm 4:4 where David said, "Tremble, and do not sin; meditate in your heart upon your bed, and be still." More literally, the original language might be translated, "Tremble with anger or fear, and do not sin; speak in your heart upon your bed, and be still."[5]

Meditation, or "speaking in your heart," is taking time to put our feelings into words, to understand what we are angry about, and to see if we can resolve our anger ourselves. It allows time for the physiological arousal that accompanies anger to calm down.

While meditating, we can ask ourselves such questions as these:

♦ Is my self-esteem being attacked?
♦ Has he really wronged me?
♦ Is this a troubled person who cannot see me in a fair light?
♦ Whom does she remind me of?
♦ Is this an area where I am extra sensitive?
♦ Am I just irritable right now?

Anger is based on what we think about a situation, and our thinking may be in error or even sinful. Meditation permits us to resolve our anger if it is really not the other person's problem or we have misunderstood the situation.

Sometimes, a calm moment to think may resolve our anger so satisfactorily that we can genuinely and graciously let the offense go by: "A man's discretion makes him slow to anger, and it is his glory to overlook a transgression" (Proverbs 19:11). But we must be sure we are honest with ourselves about the status of the anger. Is it really gone or are we just trying to convince ourselves it is so that we can remain passive?

If we cannot resolve the problem alone, a moment of meditation may help us plan how to speak tactfully but truthfully. Proverbs 15:28 points out, "The heart of the righteous ponders how to answer, but the mouth of the wicked pours out evil things."

Finally, meditation buys us time to listen to or think about the other person's point of view in order to understand it. James 1:19 urges, "But let everyone be quick to hear, slow to speak, and slow to anger." Often, we have to hear the other person's truth in love in order to speak our own truth in love. Many arguments are never resolved, because each person is fighting to be heard and no one is listening. Anger, then, is never really put away.

The passive person prefers only to go as far as meditation and avoids confrontation. As a result, he courts the danger that goes with pent-up anger. Perhaps he might habitually turn blame onto himself for any conflict (by replaying his critical tapes) and thus become abnormally depressed and suffer from guilt tapes.

What do the Scriptures say about dealing with unresolved conflict? We are to go to our brother whether we have something against him (Matthew 18:15-17) or he has something against us (Matthew 5:23-24).

If meditation does not put away anger, the next step is to speak the truth in love to the other person. We might call this act "confession" — admitting our anger without attacking the other person.

Let's see how our fictitious characters illustrate confession, or assertiveness. Notice your inner reaction.

> *Husband:* Dear, you know how we agreed that today you'd do the grocery shopping and I'd do the laundry?

> *Wife:* Yes.

> *Husband:* Well, I didn't want it to take all day. So I just threw all the light and dark clothes together in one load. Unfortunately, the colors all ran together, and your dress was ruined.

> *Wife:* Dear, when you ruin my best clothes through carelessness, I feel furious. And in the future, I definitely would like you to be more careful.

The wife said what she really thought and felt in all it's true intensity and thus, was satisfied. She had put away her anger. Do you sense that? She was honest but tactful and kind. Since she did not attack her husband's self-esteem, she did not sin, nor stir up his anger.

The wife was also direct, and therefore powerful. If her husband was crushed or angered by this, it was because he, not she, had a problem. For example, he might have had low self-esteem that made him overly sensitive to anything that sounded as if someone were displeased with him. Or he might have indulged in extreme self-preference that included a belief in his right to have whatever he wished and in the unfairness of anyone who was assertive.

A third possibility is that he might have lacked a sense of selfhood. In his insecurity, he might have been possessive of his wife, fearing that her growing self-confidence and independence would cause her to abandon him for another more mature man.

Though some people cannot respond even to assertiveness, of the four alternatives, being assertive is the most likely way of putting away anger and still affirming each person's value. If the other person cannot handle it, it is that person's problem. We have done what we could.

In the dialogue illustrating assertivenesss, I had the wife illustrate an outline I recommend for assertive expression of anger. The outline is this:

◆ When you (*summarize behavior*),
◆ I feel (*state the emotion, e.g., angry, resentful, etc.*).
◆ And in the future, I would like you to (*state the behavior*).

If you are not sure what new behavior you want, this alternative may be helpful:

◆ When you (*summarize behavior*),
◆ I feel (*state the emotion*).
◆ I don't want to feel this way toward you.
◆ Would you be willing to work with me to resolve this problem?

These are "I" statements that stick to expressing personal

truth about what "I" think and feel. By contrast, the earlier example of the wife's aggression toward her husband was full of "you" statements in which she claimed to judge what was true about him. "You" statements tend to project blame and are, therefore, often perceived as aggression, while "I" statements are usually less judgmental and, therefore, more tactful and better received.

If you are afraid to be assertive, sometimes a way to begin is to speak the truth in love about that. An example is saying, "I'm scared, but there's something I need to open up about."

A final thought. Are there even times we should not be assertive? Of course. If you feel a pointed object pressed between your shoulder blades and a voice says, "Your money or your life," you might wish to be passive. Still, if you have a black belt in karate, you might prefer to be aggressive!

As the general rule, nevertheless, Paul recommends speaking the truth in love as a means to putting away anger in personal relationships and as a means of enabling one another to grow into Christian maturity. He himself was assertive with Peter on one occasion (Galatians 2:11) and with government officials on another occasion (Acts 16:35-39).

Other examples of assertiveness in Scripture even include assertive expressions of anger between believers and God. David expressed his anger toward God even while he trusted him (Psalm 22). David's experience reminds me of a time I previously referred to when I poured out my anger at God. "Why don't you do something, God!" I prayed while shoving the couch into the wall with every syllable. At the same time I also affirmed, "God, I know you are right, but I just can't see it right now." (At a later time, I did see what he was doing.)

The ability to be assertive is crucial to self-esteem. Mastering this skill is vital to the personal maturation of competence. Dr. James Masterson, a well-known psychiatrist, says self-esteem "is based for the most part on the achievement of the capacity to utilize self-assertion to identify and activate in reality its [the whole self's] own activated thoughts, wishes, and feelings."[6]

In other words, assertiveness is using our God-created capacities as the images of God to think, to feel, to choose, to act. It is speaking up, using power appropriately (lovingly), and experiencing ourselves making an impact on others. It is living by affirming tapes based on God's Word that say, "Think," "Feel," "Talk," and "Say it in love."

## Summing It Up

It's a pretty safe guarantee that those who learn to be assertive will experience an exhilarating rise in self-esteem. Assertiveness means it's all right to be a person. It's good to face the truth about what we really think and feel. It's all right to know ourselves—both the parts of ourselves we don't like and the parts of ourselves we do like, the "old self" and the "new self." And it's positively healing to talk about all aspects of our inner selves, including our anger, when we say it in love toward ourselves and others.

It's OK to feel anger, but we should also resolve it through meditation and assertiveness. Aggression, passivity, and passive aggression don't do the job. Love and truth do.

Speaking the truth in love is one way in which we can help one another become more like Christ, Paul says. Two of the great attributes of Jesus Christ, God's Son, are truth and love. God is truth (John 14:6), and God is love (1 John 4:16). It is little wonder, then, that both the means and the goal of our Christian maturity are truth and love. We affirm the worth of ourselves, others, and God, and we become more like him when we speak the truth in love.

The next and final chapter tells why it is that love for ourselves, others, and God must go together or we cannot properly love at all.

## Target Questions

1. Which of the following degrees of anger have you personally experienced?

| Minimum | Moderate | Maximum |
|---|---|---|
| irritated | mad | hate-filled |
| annoyed | resentful | wrathful |
| aggravated | indignant | furious |
| provoked | disgusted | enraged |
| | exasperated | |

2. Choose the statement that best describes your personal belief about the value of anger. Then choose one of these statements you think is most consistent with what the Scriptures say about anger.

A. We'd all be better off without it.

B. When it comes to anger, the more the merrier. I get an enjoyable "high" from power and revenge when I let it blow.

C. It's OK to be angry about injustices done to God or others but not to oneself.

D. Anger is an unpleasant but necessary signal system that alerts us to perceived injustices.

3. Do you agree or disagree with the following statements? Why? (Refer to Ephesians 4:15-32.)

Agree   Disagree

☐      ☐      A. The emotion of anger is not sinful.

☐      ☐      B. The feeling of anger and what we actually do about it in choosing our behavior are two different matters.

☐      ☐      C. Our thinking that results in our becoming angry in a given situation might be sinful.

| Agree | Disagree | |
|---|---|---|
| ☐ | ☐ | D. It is possible to speak the truth in love about anger. |

4. What do you believe the Apostle Paul means by his phrase "speaking the truth in love" in Ephesians 4:15?

5. Below are some common sentiments about how to "put away" or resolve anger. With which one(s) do you agree? Why?

| Agree | Disagree | |
|---|---|---|
| ☐ | ☐ | A. I let people know exactly how I feel, and if they don't like the way I say it, that's just too bad. |
| ☐ | ☐ | B. Letting someone "have it" is the best way to get the anger out of your system. |
| ☐ | ☐ | C. The best solution is beating a punching bag, running a mile, playing football, or hitting golf balls while thinking of each ball as the head of someone you're mad at. |
| ☐ | ☐ | D. Christians should keep being sweet no matter what. |
| ☐ | ☐ | E. It's better to suffer than to chance getting some mad at you. |
| ☐ | ☐ | F. Talking about anger will only hurt someone. |
| ☐ | ☐ | G. Proficiency at sarcasm is good, clean sport. |

Agree   Disagree

☐    ☐    H. It's best to get someone back so indirectly that the person can't prove you did it intentionally.

☐    ☐    I. Be honest yet considerate when telling someone about your anger.

☐    ☐    J. Try to resolve your anger by privately summing up the situation accurately first. If that doesn't work, go to the person and try to talk it out.

☐    ☐    K. If the other person can't or won't talk things out, do what you can to help yourself cope, and leave your need for justice in God's hands.

6. The Scriptures strictly forbid us to take revenge into our own hands. (See Romans 12:19; Proverbs 24:17-18.) What do you think are God's reasons for this advice?

7. There are four renditions of a husband-wife scenario in this chapter. They show different ways of communicating about anger: aggression, passivity, passive aggression, and assertiveness. What were your personal emotional reactions while reading each of these? (For example, did you feel anger at one of the characters? Frustration? Admiration? Did you laugh?) Why?

8. Did you see yourself in one or more of the four ways of dealing with anger illustrated in this chapter?

Why do you think you prefer dealing with anger in that particular way? What has been satisfying about your usual patterns? And dissatisfying?

Do you intend to change? What do you plan to do differently?

9. Picture this scene. You walk into the bathroom to take a bath and discover that a member of your family has used *your* towel, which is the last clean towel, to wipe the floor. You know who did this.

As you mentally size up the situation, you conclude that there was no good excuse. Your family member was inconsiderate. You are too irritated to resolve your anger without saying something.

You plan what you will say to that person. If you use one of the outlines suggested in this chapter, what will you say?

Now imagine that you are also afraid to be assertive. This chapter suggests you initially deal with your fear by briefly speaking the truth in love about your own fear. If you try this, what will you say?

# 13
# WHAT HAPPENS WHEN I REALLY LOVE MYSELF?

Early one August morning, my husband, Terry, and I awoke to the sound of sirens, a big crash, and a voice shouting through a bull horn, "Get your hands up. Straight up!" Terry ran to the window and saw several .45's aimed in our direction. We hit the floor! After the noise abated, we ventured out of the house to discover that the police had been chasing a stolen get-away car. The youthful robbers had missed a turn and ploughed into our parked car, smashing it accordionstyle up onto the curb. Subsequently, some got away on foot, but two were caught and confined to the backseat of a police car.

The whole story, we learned, was that they had held up a local market very early that morning, had beaten the cashier within an inch of his life with a chain, and had stolen the change in the register and a six- pack of cheap ale. When the police officer finished explaining the events to us and our gathering neighbors, one of the robbers caught my husband's attention and cheerily tried to charm him into letting him out of the police car so that he could flee.

As I looked into that young man's eyes (glazed apparently due to drugs) and realized how devoid of regard for others he was, it was almost impossible for me to see any redeeming value in him. "Do I really believe he is the image of God and, therefore, has worth?" I asked myself. I thought of how many times I had told others that I believed in the immeasurable value of every human being, no matter how marred by sin. Now that belief was being tested. I knew that if unconditional love did not apply to him in his reprobate state, I could not count on it being there for me when I fall. If he did not have unchangeable worth, then neither do I.

The Scriptures seem clear that what gives me value is also what confers worth upon each and every member of the human race. Room for a double standard does not exist. I cannot have one for myself and another for others, or one for so-called good people and another for "blatant" sinners. Similar value for all stems from the same unchangeable truth: we are the image of God, who loves us and whose Son Jesus died for us. This principle is at the same time the basis for both self-love and love for others.

## Self-negation

Most of us realize the Scriptures will not allow us to affirm our own value while thinking less of others. That is no way to fulfill God's law of love. However, many Christians have accepted the reverse double standard—devaluing themselves in one theological way or another while attempting to value others—as a means of learning to love. They suppose that low self-esteem, not self-love, enables us to love others. This self-negation theory has been proposed in various forms.

*Theory One.* One version of self-negation is the *self-death,* or self-hatred, theory. According to this view, we should equate our inner selves in their entirety with the old sin nature and loathe ourselves as despicable worms. Jesus becomes all; we are nothing. (This view often includes the notion that we should see ourselves as inferior to others.) This attitude will supposedly result in humility and putting Jesus and others first.

I find this view unscriptural. Of course, as I have discussed in chapter 5, I think it is unscriptural to equate the whole inner self with the sin nature. However, besides that, the Apostle Paul makes it plain, as Dr. Vernon Grounds has pointed out, that we do and may love ourselves.[1]

*So husbands ought also to love their own wives as their own bodies. He who loves his own wife loves himself; for no one ever hated his own flesh, but nourishes and cherishes it, just as Christ also does the church, because we are members of His body. (Ephesians 5:28-30)*

Paul uses two words in the original language here to describe self-love. One is *agape,* or unconditional love, the highest form of love in the New Testament.

The other word means literally "kept warm" or figuratively "cherish" with tender love and care or "comfort."[2] Paul uses this word to describe how he tenderly cared for the Christians at Thessalonica. He said, "But we proved to be gentle among you, as a nursing mother *tenderly cares for* her own children" (1 Thessalonians 2:7, my italics). The same word was also used in a early Greek translation[3] of Deuteronomy 22:6 to describe a mother bird covering her young with her feathers to keep them warm.

Here in Ephesians 5:29, Paul uses the same word *[tenderly] cherish* to describe self-love. He clearly states that no one hates his own body, but rather nourishes and cherishes it in the very same way that Christ nourishes and cherishes Christians because we are the members of his body. This analogy is lofty and entirely positive to Paul. The motive he advances for husbands to love *(agape)* their wives is that to do so is part of what it means for husbands to love *(agape)* themselves. As Jesus Christ, in effect, loves himself by loving and cherishing Christians who are a part of him, so should a husband love himself and his wife.

Jesus also taught that we do and may love ourselves. He saw self-love as the best description for how we should love others: " 'You shall love your neighbor as yourself' " (Matthew 22:39). (Again, *agape* love is the word used.) To Jesus and Paul, self-love is not a cause for shame, fear, or guilt.

On another occasion, Jesus said that we should "hate" our family members and our own lives. The context shows what he meant—our devotion to him should be so great that our attitude toward ourselves and others, *by contrast*, will seem like hate:

> *If anyone comes to Me, and does not hate his own father and mother and wife and children and brothers and sisters, yes, and even his own life, he cannot be my disciple. Whoever does not carry his own cross and come after me cannot be My disciple.* (Luke 14:26-27)

The overwhelming theme of love in the Scriptures requires us to fit this passage to it, not the reverse.

*Theory Two.* Another self-negation approach to loving others is the *self-distrust* theory. In it, dying to self is taken to mean the annihilation of one or more parts of our God-created faculties, such as the mind, will, or emotions, which are equated with the old sin nature. I believe this, too, is an unscriptural concept, not to mention an impossible admonition. To cease to think, to choose, or to feel totally is to experience brain death or to become a human vegetable—hardly the means to becoming like Christ. The Scriptures, on the other hand, indicate we should cooperate with the Holy Spirit in transforming and purifying how we employ our God-created inner capacities.

*Theory Three.* Yet another version of the self-negation theory is a bit more subtle. It is the *self-forgetfulness*, or lack of self-awareness, approach. The idea is that, instead of loving ourselves, we should not evaluate ourselves at all. We should be so absorbed in an upward and outward focus on others that we never bother to reflect on our own value or wishes. Advocates of this view might praise someone with such words as, "She never thought of herself."

While this notion may, at first glance, seem admirable, I believe it is merely a self-negation theory revisited in different garb. Actually, I see it as yet one more approach that seeks to equate a God-created human ability with the sin nature. This time the scapegoat is not necessarily the human mind, will, or emotions. What is being devalued, even discarded, if that were possible, is our God-created capacity for self-observation, self-evaluation, and awareness of our own needs and desires. However, we can no more cease to reflect on or evaluate ourselves than we can cease to think, choose, or feel.

Thinking is an inextricable part of what we are as humans and as images of God. In fact, the ability to think about ourselves thinking is considered by developmental psychologists to be a hallmark of the most advanced levels of intellectual maturation in the human being! It is almost certainly one of the characteristics that distinguishes humans from all lower forms of life!

The Scriptures recognize our capacity for self-evaluation as good. Paul said self-evaluation was a necessary prerequisite for taking the Lord's Supper:

> But let a man examine himself, and so let him eat of the bread and drink of the cup. But if we judged ourselves rightly, we should not be judged. But when we are judged, we are disciplined by the Lord in order that we may not be condemned along with the world. (1 Corinthians 11:28, 31-32)

In other words, we must evaluate ourselves if we are to avoid being disciplined by the Lord. However, this requires thinking about, and focusing on, ourselves.

We have the capacity for self-awareness because we are God's images, and God has this capacity. In the beginning, we are told, God created and then evaluated everything he had made: "And God saw everything that He made, and behold, it was very good" (Genesis 1:31). Not only did God evaluate his behavior, but he also evaluated himself. First Peter 1:16 quotes the Old Testament Law (Leviticus 11:44-45, 19:2), saying, ". . . You shall be holy, for I am holy." God was aware of himself as an object that he evaluated as holy. Apparently, he also wants us to evaluate ourselves to see if we are becoming as holy as he is.

233

Common sense should tell us that we need to be aware of ourselves to varying degrees at different times. If we mentally review a typical day in our personal life, we will see how frequently in both subtle and obvious ways we necessarily exercise self-awareness. If we are loving and oriented toward others, we will experience a natural ebb and flow between absorption with persons and activities outside ourselves on the one hand and self-awareness on the other.

"You shall love your neighbor as yourself" implies that to whatever degree loving others requires awareness of them, loving ourselves also requires self-awareness. When we love people, we do not wish them never to think of themselves. We want them to take good care of themselves and let us know their needs. Our heavenly Father, too, wants us to make our wishes known to him (Matthew 7:7-11; Philippians 4:6; Psalm 145:19). He does not want us to never think of ourselves.

## The Failure of Self-Negation Theories

Self-negation theories have a problem in common. Telling a person who is in inner misery and torment from low self-esteem (perhaps caused in part by the self-negation theory itself) to forget himself or herself and focus on loving others is like advising a starving person to feed the poor. As wonderful as the prescribed behavior might be, the sufferer cannot do it! What is needed are steps that fall between the present problem and the desired final goal—namely, steps to self-healing.

When I was a college student, I remember sitting at my desk in my dorm room and feeling overwhelmed by a sense of loneliness. As I gazed out the window, I felt an acute need for self-love and love from another person. Someone had suggested the best way to meet my need for love was by giving to others.

Thinking about this, I glanced down at a blue-and-white candy tin decorated in the lovely Delft pattern of the Dutch. One of my dorm mates had been struck by its beauty the previous day. Even though I hated to part with it, I knew she would like having it. Besides, it was one way to follow the altruistic advice that had been given to me earlier. I reached over and picked up the tin with a sense of self-sacrifice and walked to the girl's room. She accepted the gift with much appreciation for my thoughtfulness. I, however, returned to my room with a sense of loss. My giving had not satisfied the emptiness I felt.

What this illustration shows is that giving in order to achieve love or to experience it may not work. Instead, such giving may feel like masochism or martyrdom. The end result is depletion, not completion. This kind of giving is defective because it does not flow freely from the heart or out of inner fullness.

## Learning to Love

The "more excellent way," Paul says, is the way of love. We must love first before we can truly give. Giving, even in sacrifice, is hollow without love as its motivating power. "It profits me nothing," Paul explains in 1 Corinthians 12:31-13:3.

How, then, do we learn to love? The Apostle John gives us the answer: "We love, because He first loved us" (1 John 4:19). In other words, we learn to love by experiencing *God's love*.

In order to love as God wants us to, we need to experience these biblical truths:

1. We belong to God the Father and he is close to us.

2. We are worthy because Jesus died for us.

3. We have potential to grow as we cooperate with the Holy Spirit's loving and comforting aid.

Since God loves us, we are somebodies and we are not alone. The implications of this truth are astounding:

1. When others do not recognize our value, we can recognize their error, leave our need for justice in God's hands, and let go of any painful grudges.

2. If we suffer, God has a loving purpose and we need not turn against ourselves.

235

3. If we sin, God still loves us as much as he can, which is *totally*, so that we can correct ourselves lovingly as he does.

4. Our feelings matter as much as everybody else's, and we have the right to express ourselves assertively.

When we saturate our hearts with the truths of God's love and experience a relationship with him, we can say with the Apostle John, "And we have come to know and have believed the love which God has for us. God is love, and the one who abides in love abides in God, and God abides in Him" (1 John 4:16).

Then we know, by analogy, how to love others as God has loved us and them. John says, "Beloved, if God so loved us, we also ought to love one another" (1 John 4:11). The Scriptures record the living examples of people, such as a prostitute[4] and Zaccheus,[5] who learned to love by experiencing the love Jesus had for them. From the experience of God's love come self-love, the beginning of spiritual and emotional wholeness. Love of God and others is the culmination.

## When I Love Myself the Wrong Way

Our discussion would not be complete unless I mentioned the type of self-love that does not result in the ability to love others. C. S. Lewis called this kind of love "self-preference." It is the opposite of self-negation.

The ancient Greeks epitomized self-preference in the myth of Narcissus. This exquisitely handsome lad refused to love anyone because he believed to do so would be to give someone else power over him. He broke the hearts of so many young ladies and goddesses alike that the great goddess Nemesis, whose name means "righteous anger," answered the prayer of one of the wounded. The prayer was "May he who loves not others love himself."

This prayer was answered when Narcissus bent over a clear pool to take a drink and immediately fell in love with his reflection. He was so enraptured with himself that he could not stop gazing at his own beauty mirrored in the water until he finally died. When the nymphs came to bury him, they could not find his body, but instead found a new and lovely flower, which they named Narcissus after him.[6]

Narcissus idealized himself and disregarded others. Self-preference is based, not on a given (such as God's love) that would give all people the same value, but on a changeable characteristic, such as beauty, by which we may judge ourselves to be better than others. There are other drawbacks to self-preference:

1. It may be based on a belief that others do not matter except possibly as they are useful to us. We may chiefly relate to others as extensions of ourselves, existing for our own glory and gratification.

2. We may cling to others, using them as crutches to help us function in ways we should be able to function on our own.

3. Perhaps worst of all, we might be so absorbed in ourselves that we fail to see others as persons in their own right, but only as projections of something in our mind.

The error of building self-esteem on either comparison or supposed innate superiority leads to conceit and self-elevation. Self-preference is selfishness or pride.

I once worked in a secular counseling center where many of the therapists advised people, "Live for yourself." I thought this philosophy tended to relieve people of inferiority feelings at the expense of making them selfish. One emotional problem was replaced with another.

The Apostle Paul captures the spirit of this type of selfism and hedonism:

> For men will be lovers of self, lovers of money, boastful, arrogant, revilers, disobedient to parents, ungrateful, unholy, unloving, irreconcilable, malicious gossips, without self-control, brutal, haters of good, treacherous, reckless, conceited, lovers of pleasure rather than lovers of God. . . . (2 Timothy 3:2-4)

Obviously, he is describing here a type of self-love different from the self-*agape* love we saw him depict in Ephesians

5:28-29. Significantly, the word he uses for self-love in 2 Timothy appears nowhere else in Scripture.[7] Paul is referring to a unique sort of love for self.[8] The self-love in Ephesians is godly, while the self-preference in 2 Timothy is anything but.

The proud are motivated by selfish ambition (James 3:14-16; Galatians 5:20). Money, power, and prestige are their obsession. As Brownback points out, the proud feel far more comfortable than those who suffer from low self-esteem. They are aggressive, "dominate others, get what they want (at the expense of others if necessary), and then others exalt them out of fear and respect for their wealth and power."[9] Paul's corrective is found in Galatians 5:26 and Romans 12:16: "Let us not become boastful, challenging one another, envying one another," and "Be of the same mind toward one another; do not be haughty in mind, but associate with the lowly. Do not be wise in your own estimation."

The problem with the proud and self-centered is not that they have too much self-love but the wrong kind. They do not find their glory in being God's image, but rather in the vain glory of setting themselves on pedestals as gods or of comparing themselves favorably against others and then basing their values on this comparison. "It is not good to eat much honey, nor is it glory to search out one's own glory," Proverbs 25:27 says.

It is one thing to acknowledge our strengths correctly as Paul in 1 Corinthians 11:1 and as he recommended in Romans 12:3: However, it is quite another thing to esteem ourselves better than others and to give the ultimate credit for our strengths to ourselves rather than to God. How easy it is to forget the One who gave us our capacities and opportunities for our fulfillment, but also for the service of others.

In his book *God in the Dock*, C. S. Lewis discusses two types of self-love and two kinds of self-hate. He indicates we should accept the type of self-love that regards each and every self as "God's creature, an occasion of love and rejoicing; now, indeed, hateful in condition, but to be pitied and healed."[10]

On the other hand, self-love in the form of "self-preference" is to be rejected. Similarly, he supports the type of self-hate that is the hatred of the self as preferential, the "special value of the particular self called *me*,"[11] "an irrational claim to preference."[12]

Nevertheless, Lewis warns us to beware of the self-hatred that follows from, or generalizes to, hatred of all selves. "The wrong asceticism torments the self,"[13] he says. The various self-negation theories fall into this category. If I equate myself with my sin nature and hate myself, then logically I must equate others with their sin natures and hate them, too.

In short, Lewis explains, the Christian "may hope when he has truly learned (which will hardly be in this life) to love his neighbor as himself, he may then be able to love himself as his neighbor: that is, with charity instead of partiality."[14]

Self-preference is the essence of the sin nature or of the psychological immaturity to which we must die.

## How Do I Give of Myself?

If preference is to be attributed to anyone, it is to be bestowed on others. "Be devoted to one another in brotherly love; give preference to one another in honor," the Apostle Paul commands (Romans 12:10). Now, if the same unchangeable truths bestow the same value on every person, how can we give others preference over ourselves? Precisely by *giving it*. It is our *gift* to them.

Jesus is our example, Paul says.

> *Do nothing from selfishness or empty conceit, but with humility of mind let each of you regard one another as more important than himself; do not merely look out for your own personal interests, but also for the interests of others.*
>
> *Have this attitude in yourselves which was also in Christ Jesus, Who, although He existed in the form of God, did not regard equality with God a thing to be grasped, but emptied Himself, taking the form of a bond-servant, and being made in the likeness of men.*

> *And being found in appearance as a man, He humbled Himself by becoming obedient to the point of death, even death on a cross.*
>
> *Therefore also God highly exalted Him, and bestowed on Him the name which is above every name, that at the name of Jesus every knee should bow, of those who are in heaven, and on earth, and under the earth, and that every tongue should confess that Jesus Christ is Lord, to the glory of God the Father.* (Philippians 2:3-11)

Jesus was equal with Father God, yet gave preference to the Father's will and humbled himself as a servant to the Father, even to the point of laying down his life. The Father, in turn, highly exalted Jesus. In like manner, Paul says, we are to have Jesus' attitude. We should do nothing from an attitude of self-preference, but instead, like Jesus, humbly regard others as more important than ourselves.

Jesus had the right to act like an equal with the Father, because he was equal. Hence, when he gave preference to his Father, the Father did not take it by force or dominate Jesus, who acquiesced freely and generously. It was a gift. It is in the same willing manner that we humans, who are the image of God, give preference to one another.

Jesus calls us likewise to give our lives to him:

> *And He summoned the multitude with his disciples, and said to them, "If anyone wishes to come after Me, let him deny himself, and take up his cross, and follow Me.*
>
> *"For whoever wishes to save his life shall lose it; and whoever loses his life for My sake and the gospel's shall save it.*
>
> *"For what does it profit a man to gain the whole world, and forfeit his soul?*
>
> *"For what shall a man give in exchange for his soul?"* (Mark 8:34-37)

In saying this, Jesus is not assuming that we have little value, but that we have more value than the whole world. That

Jesus wants us to invest our lives in him presupposes our value and enhances it. If we invest our lives in Christ, we will actualize ourselves (our "souls") to the fullest.

We can invest our lives in self-preference (vain glory and hedonism) or in following Christ. The first will give us tinsel; the second will yield fullness of meaning in life and eternal glory.

## What Love Accomplishes

Love is a chief trait of a mentally healthy person. When we have become perfected in love, we will be perfect.

Love fulfills the whole of God's Law and is the fruit of the Holy Spirit. When we have been perfected in love, the image of God will be fully restored in us so that we will reflect the image of Christ. "He who loves makes his human nobility real, for love is God's nature," says Sauer.[15] "The goal of the work of divine love is the new man. But this goal is not attained without man and his work of love," says Stauffer. "In love the work of God and the work of man unite."[16] It is love that gives value to all other actions (1 Corinthians 13:1-3).

Love for God and others is the basis for morality, as the two great commandments of Jesus show (Matthew 22:36-40). Recognizing this basis for morality, Augustine is said to have summed it up in this way: love God and do as you please.[17] When we are fulfilling the law of love, we will do the will or pleasure of God from the heart because it pleases us to do so.

Love satisfies and fulfills. It is joy, peace, patience, kindness, goodness, faithfulness, gentleness, and self-control. It is the true greatness of human life; it gives us power and victory. Love is purposeful living, the one authentic value in life that gives us a taste of heaven on earth.[18]

Ironically, the one who loves glorifies the beloved and is glorified himself. As important as self-esteem is, the greatest joy and goal in life is not self-esteem! It is the ability to esteem others—to love.

The old self, our sin nature, lures us to the fool's gold of self-preference, but the Holy Spirit and the new self exalt the love of God and seek to help us know more of God by loving as he loves.

## When I Love, I Worship

Earlier, we saw that loving others is loving God in effigy, since others are images of God. Similarly, loving Christians is loving Christ! The Apostle Paul learned this the hard way.

The occasion for his conversion took place while he was in the middle of an act of aggression against early Christians. God appeared to Paul, calling him by his Jewish name, Saul:

> *Now Saul, still breathing threats and murder against the disciples of the Lord, went to the high priest, and asked for letters from him to the synagogues at Damascus, so that if he found any belonging to the Way, both men and women, he might bring them bound to Jerusalem. And it came about that as he journeyed, he was approaching Damascus, and suddenly a light from heaven flashed around him; and he fell to the ground, and heard a voice saying to him, "Saul, Saul, why are you persecuting Me?" And he said, 'Who art Thou, Lord?' And He said, 'I am Jesus whom you are persecuting. . . .' "* (Acts 9:1-5)

Paul's acts of aggression against Christians were acts of aggression against Christ, whereas acts of love toward Christians are acts of love toward Christ. Jesus said, "Truly I say to you, to the extent that you did it to one of these brothers of Mine, even the least of them, you did it to Me' " (Matthew 25:40).

Love means worshiping Christ, which includes loving those who belong to him. It also means loving the lost for whom he died.

I have had the pleasure of meeting a modern-day Good Samaritan who demonstrated true Christian love—Charles Engles, an eighty-five-year-old contractor and former missionary to India for thirty-three years. He recounted to me an experience he had had in India.

One day he saw an old woman lying naked and dying beside the road. He sent a messenger to a Hindu lawyer friend who lived a block away. "Tell him, 'Charles Engles sent me and needs your cart right away. Put some straw in it and send your driver over with it.'"

The Muslim cart driver arrived and was disgusted. "What are you helping her for?" he said with a scowl.

Mr. Engles instructed him to back the cart so he himself could lift her in. Then he instructed the driver, "Take her to the government hospital as quickly as you can, but drive very carefully and see to it that she does not fall out."

He rushed ahead on foot to the hospital, there making arrangements with the chief doctor, a Hindu man whom he knew. "Give her the best food and care that you have. If it costs more than the government will pay for, send the bill to me." These instructions were carried out and the woman lived, but no bill was sent. "I guess the director would have felt too ashamed," Mr. Engles surmised.

The villagers puzzled among themselves, "Why did he do it? She was not from his family or even his tribe or country. But we came to realize that he was right, that every human being is valuable. It took a foreigner to teach us how we should treat people."

Love is a powerful means of change. When we love a person precisely because that person is God's image, we affirm the value of God and worship him. In turn, by worshiping our Lord, we focus our hearts on him and internalize his qualities, embracing them and becoming like him.

The truth that we are God's image should lead us not only to love ourselves and others, but most of all to love and worship God. When David exults in man's creation as Earthrulers who are "a little lower than God" and crowned with "glory and majesty," he begins and ends with these words: "O Lord, our Lord, how majestic is Thy name in all the earth!"

(Psalm 8). We should love the Original, the Infinite of which we are the finite image. Worship includes affirming that God belongs, is worthy or holy, and is competent or omnipotent.

Everything we do should be an act of love and hence akin to worship. We belong to God as well as to his earthly creation (in that we are both spiritual and physical beings). Moreover, our relationship to God gives our relationship to Earth its eternal and deepest significance. Our highest royal dignity as rulers of Earth and bearers of God's image comes about most completely "only by dedicating this transitory world to the service of the Eternal," says Sauer.[19] Through our worship we offer the earthly to the heavenly.

The consequences of our love for God are thus both present and eternal. While our concern has been for our present well-being—that we might live life to the full—we see that our present experiences prepare us for the ages to come.[20] To the degree that we have faith to offer ourselves to God in this life, we will reign with him now and eternally.

Wholeness in this life (as it comes from Christ) will lead to eternal glory. The one will direct us to the other. But if we are to take the road that leads to wholeness, the here and now is where we must begin.

## Target Questions

1. How do you tenderly cherish and tenderly care for yourself? To answer this question, consider your activities during the course of a day. What do you do to nourish and comfort yourself physically? Emotionally? Intellectually? Socially? Spiritually?

Are there also some things you should do to care for yourself that you neglect to do? For example, do you need more exercise, a better diet, more adequate sleep?

How well are you doing emotionally? Do you need to apply principles such as those offered in this book? Would you like to share an emotional struggle or burden with someone?

Are you spending enough time with friends, with people who are food for your soul?

Do you need more intellectual stimulation, perhaps through further reading, taking a course, or joining or forming a study group?

Are you giving yourself sufficient rest and relaxation? Do you need to play more?

Are you starved for spiritual food? Do you long to read or to study God's Word more regularly? To pray? To attend church? To join a small group fellowship?

As you have taken stock of how you wish to nourish and comfort yourself, body, soul, and spirit, have you thought of steps that are long overdue and that you chronically neglect? Will you decide to act now on what you know to be good for you?

2. If you envisioned how to better love and care for yourself while responding to the above exercise, the stage is set for you to consider how better to love your neighbor as you begin loving yourself more.

Begin with the most important person in your life. (If you don't have any, remedying that may be one of your goals.) Perhaps these special people include your spouse, your children, your parents, or your best friend.

The Apostle Paul says the people of our own households are our priority (1 Timothy 5:8). How can you better love and tenderly care for each one physically, mentally, emotionally, socially, and spiritually? Try to plan at least one specific action you will take to better love and cherish one of your loved ones.

Next, think of your Christian friends. What can you do to tenderly cherish and care for someone in your Christian community? Galatians 6:10 admonishes us to give preference to doing good to those who are of the household of faith. Is there an act of love and care that you have wanted to do but have postponed too long? Do you want to make concrete plans to do it now?

What about your neighbors who are unbelievers? Think of non-Christians with whom you rub elbows. In what ways would you like to love and cherish them, showing tender care for them? For example, are there neighbors you have yet to meet? Do you even *have* non-Christian friends? Perhaps you've been wanting to invite non-Christian neighbors or friends to your home. Would you like to turn that desire into a definite plan? Do you know of any special needs you could help meet? Do you sense they experience you as genuinely respecting and caring about them as they are?

Now consider the world at large. Jesus showed us in the parable of the Good Samaritan that even strangers and people we would not normally seek to know are our neighbors (Luke 10:25-37). Jesus said we are to touch unbelievers in our hometown, in our own geographical region, in neighboring geographical regions, and around the world (Acts 1:8). What do you believe the Lord would have you do to love and cherish unbelievers around the world? Do you have a sense of mission in some way? Would you like to pray for and give to some ministry, or even to have a ministry of your own?

Most of all, how can you love and tenderly cherish the Lord God? Do you worship him and tell him you adore him? Have you given your God-esteemed self and life to serve in his kingdom now and forever?

# FOOTNOTES

## Chapter 1

[1]I have adapted the terms *critical tapes* and *critical persons* from the transactional anaylsis terminology of "critical parent tapes" and "critical persons." Although I am not a transactional anaylst, I find some of the terminology from this school of thought to be helpful when communicating with laypersons.

[2]Maurice E. Wagner, *The Sensation of Being Somebody* (Grand Rapids: Zondervan, 1975), 161-171.

[3]John Bowlby, *Attachment* (New York: Basic Books, Inc., 1969, 1982).

[4]Used by permission. The author wishes to remain anonymous.

[5]Leon Rappaport, *Personality and Development* (Glenview, Ill.: Scott, Foresman and Company, 1972), 185-186. The original research information titled "Genesis of Level of Aspiration in Children from One and One-half to Three Years of Age" by E. Fales was reported by K. Lewis et al., in "Level of Aspiration" found in *Personality and the Behavior Disorders*, ed. J. McV. Hunt (New York: Ronald Press Company, 1944), 1:333-378.

[6]Ibid., 183.

## Chapter 2

[1]Thomas A. Harris, *I'm OK – You're OK: A Practical Guide to Transactional Analysis* (New York: Harper & Row, 1967, 1968, 1969).

[2]Newton Maloney, *Living the Answers* (New York: Abingdon Press, 1979), 15-26. Dr. Maloney credits an unknown source for coining the phrase, while he himself developed it in this book.

## Chapter 3

'Dr. Toni Grant, KABC, Los Angeles, California.

## Chapter 4

[1]Alex Haley, *Roots* (New York: Doubleday & Company, Inc., 1976).

[2]D. Miall Edwards, "Image," in *The International Standard Bible Encyclopedia*

ISBE), vol. 3, ed. James Orr et al. (Grand Rapids: Wm. B. Eerdmans Publishing Company, 1939), 1,450.

[3]L. Berkhoff, *Systematic Theology* (Grand Rapids: Wm. B. Eerdmans Publishing Company, 1941), 202-210.

[4]Edwards, "Image," *ISBE*, 3:1,450.

[5]Tim Timmons' sermon preached on December 7, 1975, at Hinson Memorial Church, Portland, Oregon. (Sermon title unknown.)

[6]Edwards, "Image," *ISBE*, 3:1,450.

[7]Berkhoff, *Systematic Theology*, 202-210.

[8]George L. Robinson, "David," in *ISBE*, 2:790.

[9]Maurice Wagner, *The Sensation of Being Somebody: Building an Adequate Self-Concept* (Grand Rapids: Zondervan, 1975), 164-167.

## Chapter 5

[1]George Armitage, *A Brief History of Hawaii* (Honolulu: Hawaiian Service, Inc., 1945, 1973).

[2]William F. Arndt and Wilbur F. Gingrich, *A Greek-English Lexicon of the New Testament and Other Early Christian Literature* (Chicago: University of Chicago Press, 1957), 128. The Greek word is a form of αχρειοψ (achreioo).

[3]Joseph Harry Thayer, *Thayer's Greek-English Lexicon of the New Testament* (Grand Rapids: Associated Publishers and Authors, Inc.), 91.

[4]From a radio script "Justice Plus" written by Ethel Barrett. Used by permission.

[5]Pastor Herb Anderson, formerly of Brethren in Christ Church, Chino, California, inspired this illustration.

[6]Dr. John Carter, my professor at Rosemead School of Psychology, translated Romans 8:1 this way.

[7]I am indebted to my author friend Joanne Feldmeth for writing and supplying this anecdote.

[8]Unfortunately, I have been unable to track down the song title, writer, or performer.

[9]C.S. Lewis, *The Abolition of Man* (New York: Macmillan Publishing Company, Inc., 1947), 88.

[10]Arndt and Gingrich, *A Greek-English Lexicon of the New Testament*, 201. The Greek word is δοκιμαζω (dokimazo).

## Chapter 6

[1]*The Septuagint* (a Greek translation of the Hebrew Old Testament).

[2]Ray Stedman, *What More Can God Say?* 2nd ed. (Ventura, Calif.: Regal Books, 1977). Used by permission.

[3]Ibid., 21.

[4]From a philosophically technical point of view, it may very well be that even free will is the result of our dependence on God and that we merely experience it as independent. Regardless, we have to exercise our wills.

[5]M. E. Speare, ed., *The Pocket Book of Verse: Great English and American Poems* (New York: Pocket Books, Inc., 1940), 254.

## Chapter 7

[1]George MacDonald, "The New Name," in *Unspoken Sermons* (New York: George Routledge & Sons, 1871), 100-117. This publication is out of print, but a copy of it is housed at McAllister Library, Fuller Theological Seminary, Pasadena, California.

[2]This example of Paul's self-estimate as it applies to sound judgment and humility was brought to my attention by J. Vernon Grounds' lecture "Death to the Self: Misconceptions of the Regenerating Miracle" delivered January 5, 1985. It was the second lecture in a series of three entitled "Unselfing the Self: A Pivotal Problem in Psychology and Theology," presented for the 14th Annual John G. Finch Symposium on Psychology and Theology, January 1984, Fuller Graduate School of Psychology, Pasadena, California.

[3]Paul Brownback, *The Danger of Self-Love* (Chicago: Moody Press, 1982), 143. Brownback has some good points to make about the danger of elevating one's value above that of others. Unfortunately, he makes the error of equating this type of pride with self-esteem and misses the value of understanding and ex-periencing the value God gives us.

[4]David H. Roper, *New Covenant in the Old Testament* (Waco, Tex.: Word Books, 1976), 87.

[5]Eve Curie, *Madame Curie: A Biography*, trans. Vincent Sheean (Garden City: Doubleday, Doran & Company, Inc., 1937), 304.

[6]Robert Schuller, *Self-Esteem: The New Reformation* (Waco, Tex.: Word Books, 1982), 115.

[7]Dr. Maurice E. Wagner shared this interpretation of 2 Corinthians 13:14 with me in a private conversation.

## Chapter 8

[1]The fact that Jesus experienced depression was first brought to my attention by Tim Timmons in a sermon he preached on December 7, 1975, at Hinson Memorial Church in Portland, Oregon. (Sermon title unknown.)

[2]I owe this analogy to George Martindale, Ph.D., ABPP.

[3]E. Stanley Jones, *Victory through Surrender: Self-Realization through Self-Surrender* (Nashville: Abingdon Press, 1980), 42-43.

[4]Corrie ten Boom and John Sherrill, *The Hiding Place* (New York: Bantam Books, Inc., 1974).

[5]Corrie ten Boom and Jennie Buckingham, *Tramp for the Lord* (Old Tappan, N.J.: Fleming H. Revell Company, 1974).

## Chapter 9

[1]John F. Kennedy, *Profiles in Courage* (New York: Pocket Books, Inc., 1955), 30.

[2]Ibid., 30-31.

[3]Ibid., 31.

[4]Ibid.

[5]Ibid.

[6]Nathan S. Kline, *From Sad to Glad*, rev. ed. (New York: Ballantine Books, 1974), chapter 4.

[7]Ibid., 9-12.

[8]Aaron T. Beck et al., *Cognitive Therapy of Depression* (New York: The Guilford Press, 1979), 1, 355.

[9]Ibid.

[10]Ibid., 14-15, 261. I have adapted examples from Beck et al. to my illustrations.

[11]Claudia Black, *It Will Never Happen to Me* (Denver: M.A.C. Printing and Publications Division, 1981). This secular book is excellent reading for children of alcoholics who have grown to be adolescents or adults.

[12]Beck et al., *Cognitive Therapy of Depression*, 361.

[13]Ibid.

[14]Katharine Dalton, *Once a Month* (Claremont, Calif.: Hunter House, Inc., 1983).

[15]Beck et al., *Cognitive Therapy of Depression*, 359. Further information about manic-depression may be found in Ronald R. Fieve, *Moodswing: The Third Revolution in Psychiatry* (New York: Bantam Books, 1975).

[16]Aaron T. Beck, "New Directions in Cognitive Therapy—A Day with Aaron Beck," seminar at the University of California, Irvine, University Extension, February 24, 1983.

[17]Beck et al., *Cognitive Therapy of Depression*, 356.

[18]Ibid., 390-396.

[19]Kline, *From Sad to Glad*, 15-29.

## Chapter 10

[1]Karl Menninger, *Whatever Became of Sin?* (New York: Hawthorn Books, Inc., 1973), 1-2.

²Bruce Narramore and Bill Counts, *Freedom from Guilt* (Irvine, Calif.: Harvest House, 1976). Also see S. Bruce Narramore in his book *No Condemnation* (Grand Rapids: Zondervan, 1984).

³Sidney M. Jourard, "Chapter 8: Conscience and Guilt in Healthy Personality" in *Personal Adjustment: An Approach through the Study of Healthy Personality* (New York: Macmillan, 1963).

⁴Lester David, "The Many Faces of Guilt," *Family Health / Today's Health*, July 1977. Reprinted by U.S. Government Printing Office (Washington, D.C., 1981), 341-166/6336. DHHS Publication No. (ADM) 81-580.

⁵Robert R. King, Ph.D., clarified this specific thought for me in a helpful way when he spoke on "Guilt: The Overworked Emotion" for Los Angeles area members of the Western Region, Christian Association for Psychological Studies meeting at Fuller Graduate School of Psychology, Pasadena, California, February 23, 1982.

## Chapter 11

¹William F. Arndt and Wilbur F. Gingrich, *A Greek-English Lexicon of the New Testament and Other Early Christian Literature* (Chicago: University of Chicago Press, 1957), 267. The Greek word is 'εϑοχος (henochos).

²Ibid., 852. The Greek word is 'ϑποδιχος (hupodikos).

³Ibid., 603. The Greek word is 'οϱειλο (opheilo).

## Chapter 12

¹I have discovered that the concept of "speaking the truth in love" as an ideal definition of assertiveness was also recognized by Jerry Schmidt in *You Can Help Yourself* (Irvine, Calif.: Harvest House Publishers, 1978), 47. The idea was first suggested to me by Donald F. Tweedie, Jr., Ph.D., formerly of Fuller Graduate School of Psychology, most recently at Palm Springs Psychological Services.

²From the Ann Landers column, April 8, 1969, as published in the *Wisconsin State Journal*. Copyright by Publishers-Hall Syndicate. Quoted in Leonard Berkowitz, "The Case for Bottling Up Rage," *Psychology Today*, July 1973, 24, 26.

³Leonard Berkowitz, *Aggression: A Social-Psychological Analysis* (New York: McGraw Hill Book Company, Inc., 1962).

⁴I thank Donald F. Tweedie, Jr., Ph.D., for this insight.

⁵See NASB margin notes.

⁶James F. Masterson, *The Narcissistic and Borderline Disorders: An Integrated Developmental Approach* (New York: Brunner/Mazel, 1981), 103.

## Chapter 13

¹Vernon Grounds, "Self-Love and Self-Fulfillment." Third lecture in the series

"Unselfing the Self: A Pivotal Problem in Psychology and Theology." Fourteenth Annual John G. Finch Symposium on Psychology and Theology, January 4-6, 1984, Fuller Graduate School of Psychology, Pasadena, California.

[2] William F. Arndt and Wilbur F. Gingrich, *A Greek-English Lexicon of the New Testament and Other Early Christian Literature* (Chicago: University of Chicago Press, 1957), 351. The Greek word is θαλπω (thalpō).

[3] Deuteronomy 22:6 in the *Septuagint*. See discussion of *cherish* in W.E. Vine, *An Expository Dictionary of New Testament Words*, vol. 1, (Old Tappan, N.J.: Fleming H. Revell Company), 184.

[4] Luke 7:36-50.

[5] Luke 19:1-10.

[6] Edith Hamilton, *Mythology: Timeless Tales of Gods and Heroes* (New York: The New American Library of World Literature, Inc., 1940, 1942), 87-88.

[7] Arndt and Gingrich, *A Greek-English Lexicon of the New Testament*, 866. The Greek word is φιλαντος (philautos).

[8] Henry George Liddell and Robert Scott, *A Greek-English Lexicon*, 9th ed., revised and augmented by Henry Stuart Jones (Oxford: Clarendon Press, 1940), 1,932. In extrabiblical literature φιχαμτας means "loving oneself," and may be used in a good sense, although more often it is used in a bad sense, meaning "selfish."

[9] Paul Brownback, *The Danger of Self-Love: Re-Examining a Popular Myth* (Chicago: Moody Press, 1982), 132.

[10] C. S. Lewis, *God in the Dock: Essays on Theology and Ethics*, ed. Walter Hooper (Grand Rapids: William B. Eerdmans Publishing Company, 1970), 194.

[11] Ibid., 194-195.

[12] Ibid., 194.

[13] Ibid., 195.

[14] Ibid., 194.

[15] Erich Sauer, *The King of the Earth: The Nobility of Man according to the Bible and Science* (Grand Rapids: Wm. B. Eerdmans Publishing Company, 1962), 109.

[16] Ethelbert Stauffer, "Jesus: The New Demand" (44-48) and "The Apostolic Period" (49-53). Entries under 'αγαπαω, 'αγαπη, 'αγαπηιος (21-55) in Gerard Kittel, ed., *Theological Dictionary of the New Testament, Volume I*, trans. and ed. Geoffrey W. Bromiley (Grand Rapids: Wm. B. Eerdmans Publishing Company, 1964). See page 50 especially.

[17] Augustine, *Homilies of St. John*, VII, 8. "Love and do what you will."
Augustine certainly seemed to believe morality is based on the love of all selves—love of God, self, and neighbor—and he said the love of God, love of self, and love of neighbor are closely interrelated. "But as this divine Master indicates two precepts—the love of God and the love of our neighbor—and as in these precepts a man finds three things he has to love—God, himself, and his

neighbor – and that he who loves God loves himself thereby, it follows that he must endeavor to get his neighbor to love God, since he is ordered to love his neighbor as himself." Augustine, *The City of God*, from Book XIX, chapter 14, in *The Works of Aurelius Augustine*, ed. Marcus Dods (Edinburgh: T. & T. Clark Company, 1871–1876).

[18]Sauer, *The King of the Earth*, 108.

[19]Ibid., 91.

[20]Matthew 25:14-30, Ephesians 1:20-23; 2:6-7.